The Anatomy of
Ethical Leadership

The Anatomy of Ethical Leadership

To Lead Our Organizations in a Conscientious and Authentic Manner

Lyse Langlois

Translated by Della Marcus

AU PRESS

Copyright © 2011 by Lyse Langlois
Published by AU Press, Athabasca University
1200, 10011 – 109 Street, Edmonton, AB T5J 3S6

ISBN 978-1-897425-74-9 (print)   978-1-897425-75-6 (PDF)
      978-1-926836-35-5 (epub)

Originally published as *Anatomie du leadership éthique: Pour diriger
nos organisations d'une manière consciente et authentique* (copyright
© Les Presses de l'Université Laval, 2008).

Cover and interior design by Rod Michalchuk.
Printed and bound in Canada by Marquis Book Printers.

Library and Archives Canada Cataloguing in Publication

Langlois, Lyse, 1964–
      The anatomy of ethical leadership : to lead our organizations
in a conscientious and authentic manner / Lyse Langlois.

Translation of: Anatomie du leadership éthique.
Includes bibliographical references.
Also issued in electronic format.
ISBN 978-1-897425-74-9

      1. Work ethic. 2. Leadership—Moral and ethical aspects.
3. Decision making—Moral and ethical aspects. 4. Industrial relations.
I. Title.

HD4905.L3513 2011   174'.4   C2010-907332-0

We acknowledge the financial support of the Government of Canada through
the Canada Book Fund (CBF) for our publishing activities.

 Canadian   Patrimoine
Heritage   canadien

To my friend William Hatcher,
mathematician and philosopher

It is possible to so adjust one's self to the practice of nobility that its atmosphere surrounds and colors all our acts. When these acts are habitually and consciously adjusted to noble standards with no thought of the words that might herald them, then nobility becomes the accent of life. At such a degree of evolution one scarcely needs to try to be good any longer—all our deeds are the distinctive expression of nobility.

—'Abdu'l-Bahá, *Star of the West* 17: 286

Contents

Foreword

IT IS A PLEASURE TO write a foreword to this book by Professor Lyse Langlois. I have been following her work for over a decade now, and I am increasingly impressed by her dedication to deepening her own understanding within the field of ethics, as well as by her commitment to engaging in a long-range research effort to illuminate a process of ethical decision making. I believe the present book admirably reflects both aspects of her scholarly work.

The Anatomy of Ethical Leadership helps to situate the reader within historical developments in philosophy and social theory at a time when three hundred or more years of modernity finds itself challenged by recent proponents of postmodernity. Langlois reflects her broad reading of the sources in proposing that scholars of ethics and ethical leadership are currently experiencing an overlapping of perspectives from both traditions. There is therefore a need to consider the value of perspectives offered by modernity as well as by postmodernity. Her discussion in the first part of the book enables us to situate recent developments in the field of ethics within their proper historical context. Later on, readers will see how her empirical findings tend to confirm the existence of these overlapping perspectives among educational leaders.

The second part of the book presents a broad view of leadership, attempting to ground it in a philosophical anthropology that offers reasonable interpretive frameworks, as opposed to ironclad definitive rational arguments. Her presentation of leadership as involved with ethically charged situations enables her to bring the crucial activity of decision making to the forefront of leadership action.

With the foundational landscape well articulated, Langlois moves with assurance into a description of the model that she has developed and refined for almost ten years, the trajectory of ethical, responsible, and authentic leadership (TERA). The model incorporates the complementary ethics of critique, justice, and care. In the early 1990s, I had proposed that these three ethical perspectives needed to be brought into an interdependent model of ethical reasoning in the area of educational leadership. Professor Langlois then took on the task of documenting the presence of these three ethical perspectives in the decision making of the subjects she studied. Beyond that, however, she has been able to create an ongoing learning process that has enabled these same leaders to grow in their ability to employ the three ethics intentionally and with greater sensibility in their work. She is now able to document, as well, how their enhanced facility with ethical analysis and decision making can translate into the building of an intentional ethical culture in their organizations.

This groundbreaking work offers not only to educational leaders but also to leaders in other organizations opportunities to reflect afresh on their own process of ethical decision making. It is my hope that the work of Professor Langlois will continue to gain international recognition, not only though the use of the TERA model and the documentation of its effectiveness but also by prompting more ambitious developments with other organizations.

Robert J. Starratt
Boston College

Preface and Acknowledgements

To EXPLORE SUCH A SUBJECT as ethical leadership means to discover the inner road taken by men and women who participated in my research projects—a road littered with doubts, hesitations, and reconsideration, along which they had to confront the fear of judgment but also experienced the joy of having done something to improve things around them. I am indebted to them for the precious time they dedicated to me in unveiling their ethical dilemmas. In fact, to examine and talk about an ethical dilemma, while attempting to highlight the good as well as the bad, is not easy. To broach delicate subjects regarding an organization is sometimes inconvenient and can even be quite destabilizing. To speak of fraud, sexual and moral harassment, conflicts of interest, issues surrounding maternity leave, favouritism, and internal politics that work to the detriment of justice is to raise very sensitive questions, rarely openly discussed inside an organization and even less so in the public arena. I am deeply grateful to those who opened up to me, because their confidence helped me to understand better how the exercise of ethical leadership can resolve difficult situations and can lead to lasting change in an organization.

I would also like to take this opportunity to thank Fernand Morin, professor emeritus in the Faculty of Social Sciences at Université Laval, Claire Lapointe, director of the Centre for Research on Scholastic Success at Université Laval, and Jerry Starratt, professor in the Lynch School of Education at Boston College, for their careful reading and their very relevant commentaries that helped me to improve this book, which was first published in French. My thanks also go to Paul Begley, of Penn State University, who made my year of study and research there very pleasant. Our exchanges on ethics were very enriching. I do hope we will carry on this research in collaboration. I likewise wish to thank Frédéric Lenoir, renowned philosopher, for the time he spent with me during his holiday in the summer of 2005 in Lavandou, France. His assistance helped me to clarify my ethical approach.

Very special thanks also to Della Marcus, who translated the manuscript with much patience and professionalism; to Juliette, who generously translated all the quotations on the eve of a holiday; and to Charlotte, for all her assistance.

I would also like to thank the members of the various research teams at CSRH (Conseil de recherche en sciences humaines) and IRSST (Institut de recherche en santé et en sécurité du travail) with whom I have had the pleasure of working: Claire L., Alain, Fernande. Their many questions pushed me to clarify my thinking and refine my various research tools. My gratitude goes also to Deirdre Smith, manager of the Standards of Practice and Education Unit at the Ontario College of Teachers, and to Jacky Tremblay, director of human resources at Québec's Commission scolaire des Découvrers. These two colleagues provided invaluable support during the evaluation of the TERA model in the work environment.

Of course, the writing of a work requires the time and patience of the author, but also a great deal of understanding on the part of those who are dear to the author. Work on this book began during the last six months of my year of study and research in 2005 and finished only in the fall of 2007. My family provided constant motivation, which helped me overcome obstacles along the way.

How many times did I hear my daughters, Catherine and Beatrice, ask: "Mother, is your book finished?" And how often did I have to reply: "Not yet . . ."? I thank them for waiting patiently for me to return to a normal life, in which we have time to play together again. My gratitude also goes to Daniel, an eternal optimist who, unlike myself, never doubted my abilities. And I thank Paulette for the many documents she collected and never failed to forward to me with infinite patience.

This work is dedicated to my friend William Hatcher, philosopher and mathematician, who passed away too soon and with whom I was often able to engage in an exchange on the moral dimension, the ethical decision-making process in general, and the TERA model in particular. Aside from our discussions, unfortunately far too brief, which I always considered a veritable source of intellectual inspiration, what impressed me most were his qualities of heart. Always at the service of others, he practiced a leadership marked by authentic and responsible ethics. I miss this inspiring man very deeply.

Lyse Langlois
27 November 2007

Introduction

To SEEK TO WRITE A BOOK about leadership might seem audacious, especially if one considers the thousands of scientific and professional works that already exist on the subject, some of them written by well-known authors such as Peter Drucker, Daniel Goldman, John Kotter, Abraham Zaleznik, and Peter Senge. The distinctive nature of the subject in question, namely, ethical leadership in particular, prompted me to rise to the challenge.

During my doctoral studies, at the beginning of the 1990s, I decided to delve deeper into this concept by looking initially at whether Quebec's school managers were practicing their leadership with a certain ethical dimension. Later, with the aid of research grants from FQRSC (Fonds québécois de la recherche sur la société et la culture) and from CRSH (Conseil de recherches en sciences humaines), I was able to follow up my analysis with a variety of leaders, mostly from the public sector.

My reflections took root in a Canadian context and are based especially on public sector managers working in education and in health. To date, I have interviewed over two hundred men and women with the goal of defining the contours of ethical leadership exercised in a situation of moral dilemma. Notions such as ethical sensitivity, professional judgment, and responsibility lie at the heart of this leadership. Of course, I cannot claim that the characteristics of an ethical decision outlined in this book are applicable to other environments and cultures. To draw more general conclusions, it would, of course, be necessary to carry out scientific research on diverse groups of people.

This book broadly traces the architecture of ethical leadership that I was able to observe in the individuals I interviewed. As I sought to construct an ethical model, I attempted to explain what ethical leadership is, and I endeavoured to understand the many challenges to its application in the workplace. Ethical questions are increasingly in evidence in scientific literature, especially since the 1990s. The demand for ethical leadership is fuelled by a variety of social elements: scandals of all sorts, issues arising from scientific advances, practices lacking in probity, and innovations in nanotechnologies, among others. For some, the notion of ethical leadership seems a utopia, owing to such current trends as the growth of a free market economy, the quest for performance without regard for the human element, individualistic patterns of behaviour, and complete disregard for environmental consequences.

My research led me to conclude, however, that ethical leadership is alive and well and that it takes various forms. It can be tinted by legal and regulatory frameworks, in conformity with established norms; it can be coloured by a desire to create a more human organization, in the pursuit of greater social justice; it can be imbued with personal moral values that drive conduct and decisions.

Seeking to practice ethical leadership can give the impression of swimming against the current of a society bent on a cult of performance and the logic of personal interest. To actualize ethical leadership requires repositioning ourselves towards a more positive conception of human nature. Ethical leadership challenges the conscience of the individual by inviting reflection on the actions to be taken and the commitment to an ethical perspective. Ethical leadership makes no noise, but it leaves its marks.

My reflections are based particularly on research carried out since I completed my doctoral thesis. My ideas have been refined by exchanges with other researchers working in this field and by discussions with my students in a seminar on ethics and decision making. The students not only contributed their own ideas to the developing body of knowledge on the concept, but they also pushed me to clarify my thinking further and to root it in daily life. I thank them with all my heart.

This work does not claim to be the most exhaustive of all the studies carried out on ethical leadership and the ethical decision-making process. Rather, it attempts to lay bare the facts by sorting, simplifying, and ordering the existing mass of data in order to delineate the contours of ethical leadership, to map its exercise in a decision-making process, and to understand its tensions in the workplace. This book offers a synthesis of all the interviews, field surveys, and research I have carried out on ethical leadership and decision making over the past ten years. Having already written articles that draw on the interviews I conducted, I wanted, in this book, to extract the substance of those interviews and combine it with various research data in order to provide a bigger picture. The organizing principle here turns on one central question: How does ethical leadership practice, define, and shape the ethical decision-making process?

This book presents the comments and ideas of recognized authors but also of the students and experienced managers who attended my seminars on ethical decision making. What they had to say inspired me greatly. Unfortunately, I could include only a few of their observations here, although I will retain the rest for future writing projects.

The individuals I interviewed offer a glimpse into all our struggles with our current society—its uncertainty, its transitory nature, the pressures of the market economy—and their ethical reflections and existential questioning point to new values emerging from this struggle. Faced with this realization, I thought it best to localize the questions on the basis of two currently colliding trends, namely the modern and the postmodern. Without dwelling at length on the philosophical foundations of these trends, I will attempt to draw out from the interviews elements that bring significant tension into professional life. Accordingly, I would propose the following epistemological division: the modern tradition, which sees the world through the prism of instrumental rationality, followed by a postmodern outlook that shatters the traditional notion of rationality. These thinking patterns will allow us to focus our vision of leadership and to describe the development of ethical preoccupations within leadership in broad terms.

CHAPTER 1

Modernity

An Instrumental Rationality

IN ORDER TO UNDERSTAND THE rise of ethical leadership properly, we must first focus on the period known as the managerial revolution, which, at the time, presented a specific concept of the way in which individuals should be managed within organizations. Inspired by the positivist paradigm, this revolution ensured a vision of rationality based exclusively on the economy. James Burnham announced the advent of this managerial revolution in 1941, which he claimed marked the end of the domination of capitalists, who would be replaced in the economic sphere by managers. In *The Managerial Revolution*, Burnham heralded the beginning of the era of rationalization that would usher in a form of planned social relationships within organizations. A series of management tools were then developed to allow managers to exert more effective control over individuals in their organizations and to improve performance at work in order to increase productivity. This is how utilitarian instrumentalism entered human resources. However, this approach, which is still in effect today, has proved to have weaknesses that have become increasingly evident to researchers (March and Simon 1958; Foster 1980; Greenfield 1981).

Thomas Kuhn, in *The Structure of Scientific Revolutions* (originally published in 1962), was one of the first to highlight the cracks in the model developed in modern times, namely the positivist paradigm.[1] Positivism, as developed by André Comte-Sponville, postulated that individuals could free themselves from certain preconceived notions that bound them to illusions that obstructed their understanding of things.

The Impact of Descartes and Kant on the Concept of Free Will

By taking a step further into the past, we discover that we owe to René Descartes (1596–1650) the idea of freedom of thought, liberated from suppositions and myths. With his famous *cogito ergo sum* (I think, therefore I am), Descartes would play a major part in this flow of ideas by adding reflexive consciousness to the notion of the free subject. Immanuel Kant (1724–1804) followed this trajectory by stating that enlightenment "is the human being's emergence from his self-incurred minority. Minority is the inability to make use of one's own understanding without direction from another. This minority *is self-incurred* when its cause lies not in a lack of understanding but rather a lack of resolution and courage to use this without direction from another" (Kant 1996 [1784], 17).

Descartes provides a rational basis for the concept of a universal source of knowledge founded on the mathematical model, thereby establishing the epistemological standard of science. For Georg Wilhelm Friedrich Hegel (1770–1831), Descartes is the philosopher-founder of modernity and of a rationality freed from superstition. Reason was to express itself by way of scientific knowledge, by postulating the equality of all men[2] and the existence of free will and autonomy, and by demanding democracy as a way of governing oneself.

---

1. In Kuhn's usage, the term *paradigm* refers to a set of scientific practices. It is, in a way, a system of representations widely accepted by a community within a particular field. Paradigms thus tend to differ depending on the social group in question and to change over time in accordance with the evolution of knowledge.

2. I use the term *men* deliberately, as there was no talk of the equality of men and women at the time.

This concept was to reach its climax and have an impact on society as a whole with the advancement of the sciences. The epochal element of the positivist vision was to attempt to reduce all phenomena to a single causality and to attribute neutrality to these same phenomena in the name of scientific rationality. Questions that explore the *why*, namely, those that attempt to explore the root causes of things, are excluded from this vision. The main questions are limited to the *how*, that is, to questions formulated in terms of the laws of nature, often expressed in mathematical language. Through observation and repeated experience, this form of questioning is intended to identify relationships underlying observed phenomena that can explain the reality of facts. In some ways, this cult of reason follows a rational process of highly instrumental induction. This superstructure, which profoundly influenced Western thought and the Anglo-Saxon world, culminated in a paradigmatic revolution that was largely accepted until its re-examination in the 1960s.

Paradigm Shift: Towards Postmodernity

The work of Kuhn, among its other merits, highlighted the mental models that governed the thinking of scientists. Because they are based exclusively on mathematical thinking, these models exclude certain axioms that are required for a full understanding of reality. Indeed, the positivist model does not explain everything and, in particular, ignores the search for meaning. The re-assessment of the positivist model has not, however, led to the disappearance of this conception of rationality, which is still present in the form of neo-positivism. It is currently being put to the test against the complexity of today's world. A positivist spirit subsists in certain habits of thought and in the structures that this trend put into place. Its legacy can be seen in the technical, legal, and administrative rationality that directs our relationships with others, as well as our way of thinking. Reasoning exclusively oriented towards this type of rationality results in fragmented and restrictive thinking that lacks any understanding of interdependency. Why, then, should we be surprised by our difficulties in finding new solutions for today's ills? The re-examination of the positivist model clearly demonstrates the limitations of such reasoning (see Senge and Gauthier 1991; Morin 1999; Argyris and Schön 1996).

Rationality: Caught Between Two Worlds

We are forced to observe that the presuppositions initially excluded from the positivist vision, as well as the spiritual and axiological dimensions, sometimes reappear in the form of major crises that society must bear.[3] These missing dimensions—the return of the spiritual, the rise of ethics, and the place of values—return full force, raising numerous questions and stirring debate. For many people, these non-mathematical dimensions are annoying because they are difficult to understand and control. Rather than initiate a dialogue on these aspects of life, we neglect them or find ways to camouflage them in the name of technical rationality. These dimensions cannot be expressed as equations, however; they call on another form of logic, one that includes tensions and paradoxes. One of our present challenges is that of responding to ethical questions raised particularly by advancing biotechnologies and by environmental concerns. This ethical questioning manages to impose itself while also causing us to lose our bearings somewhat; the divide between the *why* and the *how* becomes increasingly complex and uncertain.

To illustrate this way of thinking, we can take the case of an organization. It is easier to define an organization by what it does—its behaviour, its function, its procedures (namely the *how*)—than by what lies beyond the public veneer—its internal structure, its relationships, its interactions, its overall purpose (in other words, the *why*). It is rare to find descriptions of organizations that pertain

---

3. This brings to mind the wars that are being fought around the globe in the name of religious fundamentalism, as well as the values increasingly being espoused by groups such as anti-globalizationalists, environmentalists, and ecologists. The situation we now see translates a crisis by reappropriating certain values in the name of greater social justice.

to modes of adaptation, to connections, and to suitability in terms of context and environment because such things resist the logic of a simple causal explanation. Addressing these other dimensions allows for an examination of the organization that takes into account its multifinality and the complexity of reality.[4] About reality, Paul Watzlawick states:

> Everyone develops an idea of the real. In scientific and political discourse, in everyday discussions, we defer to the supreme referent in the final analysis: reality. But where is this reality? And more importantly, does it really exist? Of all illusions, the most perilous consists in believing that there is only a single reality. In fact, there are different versions of reality, some of which are contradictory, and all of which are by-products of communication, rather than the reflection of objective and eternal realities. (1976, 41)

This complexity of the real highlights the various levels of organizational reality. The first of these is the physical or material level of being, of facts and of objects. This first level is that of objective reality, visible and quantifiable. The second level, or the social level, which derives from the former, is a psychic reality devoted to meanings and value and to organizing the categories and systems of the preceding objective reality. A fact becomes an event only by its effects and repercussions in people's minds. This same fact is recorded in the organizational memory. The third level, or the cultural level, relates to the symbolic reality of beliefs and rules that direct and delimit the meanings and value of objective reality. This level distinguishes true from false, normal from pathological, beautiful from ugly, acceptable from unacceptable, and just from unjust. Of course, bureaucratic reality must be added to these realities, in which the real is recorded in official documents.

---

4. The term *multifinality*, which comes from Anthony Wilden, refers to the fact that the same causes can produce different effects owing either to a *diversity* of levels that can be distinguished on the basis of logical type, constraints, or dependence, or to the variety of elements at each level. Diversity is a breakdown of distinct levels. This is, in a sense, the search for a meaning to be reconstructed.

The complexity thus generates a certain diversity, in the form of distinctive levels of reality, and sparks off a variety of structural arrangements and behaviours. This complexity, very much in evidence today, distinguishes itself from a binary vision in which contrasts reign. We are located here in universes that are sometimes hard to measure—that emerge in a sort of flux and in contrasts that are more or less capable of being reconciled. These universes exist side by side, sometimes sitting rather uneasily with one another. Often a single point of view is privileged, namely, that of financial viability.

Vincent de Gaulejac (2005) focuses attention on this vision that permeates organizations. Most managers go to extremes in their pursuit of financial viability, in their need to please shareholders as well as safeguard their own positions. They find it easy to switch from a mode of administration that treats people like human beings to one that considers human resources to be entirely at the service of the enterprise, much like any other type of resource or raw material. This concept destroys the meaning of any human action that attempts to open itself up to other rationalities.

Organizations that apply such logic should not be surprised to see the commitment of their employees lessen to a similarly utilitarian level, one of purely contractual relations with the business. This situation cannot persist without repercussions to the health and families of the workers. We have only to consider the increasing number of cases of professional exhaustion, a malaise often associated with increasing workload and with a significant loss of purpose, as well as with a decline in the feeling of belonging, manifested in wavering loyalty to the organization. These symptoms reflect the priorities that large businesses most often privilege. Such businesses dictate a certain vision of how organizations should be run, one that denies complexity. As a result, a sort of apathy has set in, destroying the ability of employees to use their own judgment. It is sometimes surprising to observe the extent to which individuals become paralyzed by a lack of principles with which to explain decisions. They can become very dependent on the judgment of the board of directors or of the organizational hierarchy itself. This is not to incite organizational delinquency, but there does appear to be a sort of generalized inability to think for oneself, an inability that can be produced by a lack of criteria for judgment. In a study carried out in one of the major private sector engineering companies (Lamonde et al. 2007), I noticed a certain *caution* when it came to ethical dilemmas and the question of which decision to take. As a matter of routine, validation had to pass along the hierarchical path. Engineers were often given great decision-making latitude; in times of difficulty, however, this seemed to diminish, as the hierarchy did not allow individuals the freedom to exercise their ability to judge. This can be explained, in part, by the desire for a consistent and standardized set of practices, which essentially demands that one exercise a sort of lowest-common-denominator reasoning, one that disregards the specific contexts in which people function.

Table 1, taken from de Gaulejac, highlights the main paradigms being promoted in managerial theories and by schools of administration, which guide behaviour in the workplace. This managerial power, which de Gaulejac criticizes so forcefully, has a manipulative range in accordance with terms acknowledged and accepted by all. He very rightly points out that we have moved from disciplinary power to managerial power, from control of the body to the mobilization of desire, from set working hours to an unlimited investment of one's self, from following orders to commitment to a project (2005, 83–87). From this critique of the managerial power that prevails in our organizations, we cannot leave out the direction given to leadership that, now yoked to this power, exists to serve a neoliberal ideology. Writing about global financial markets, in which companies now find their performance constantly scrutinized by investors, Pierre Bourdieu comments:

> Subjected to this permanent threat, the corporations themselves have to adjust more and more rapidly to the exigencies of the markets, under penalty of "losing the market's confidence," as they say, as well as the support of their stockholders. The latter, anxious to

Table 1: Main Paradigms in Administration

PARADIGM	BASIC PRINCIPLE	MODE OF CRITIQUE
Objectivist	To understand is to measure, to calculate	Logic based on the primacy of mathematical language above all other languages
Functionalist	The organization is a given	Logic that obscures the issues of power
Experimental	The objectification of the individual is a guarantee of the primacy of the scientific	Logic based on instrumental rationality
Utilitarian	Reflection is at the service of action	Logic subjected to the knowledge of the criteria of usefulness
Economist	The individual is a factor in the enterprise	Logic based on reducing the employee to a resource of the enterprise

SOURCE: Translated from de Gaulejac 2005, 57.

obtain short-term profits, are more and more able to impose their will on managers, using financial directorates to establish the rules under which managers operate and to shape their policies regarding hiring, employment, and wages. Thus, the absolute reign of flexibility is established, with employees being hired on fixed-term contracts or on a temporary basis, and repeated corporate restructurings and, within the firm itself, competition among autonomous divisions as well as among teams forced to perform multiple functions. Finally, this competition is extended to individuals themselves, through the individualisation of the wage relationship. (1998, 3)[5]

---

5. "Les entreprises elles-mêmes, placées sous une telle menace permanente, doivent s'ajuster de manière de plus en plus rapide aux exigences des marchés; cela sous peine, comme l'on dit, de « perdre la confiance des marchés », et, du même coup, le soutien des actionnaires qui, soucieux d'obtenir une rentabilité à court terme, sont de plus en plus capables d'imposer leur volonté aux managers, de leur fixer des normes, à travers les directions financières, et d'orienter leurs politiques en matière d'embauche, d'emploi et de salaire. Ainsi s'instaure le règne absolu de la flexibilité, avec les recrutements sous contrats à durée déterminée ou les intérims et les « plans sociaux » à répétition, et, au sein même de l'entreprise,

This state of affairs persists, and is indeed rarely contested, because a false rationale exists to justify it, one that is for the most part left unchallenged. In order to support its cause, this technical rationality allies itself with an arsenal of tools that serve to quantify what a manager is supposed to do and to help him list the qualities he must possess. This leadership is exercised exclusively within the framework of financial performance, in the service of a market economy that promises us posterity and human happiness. (For instance, the shift of direction in educational institutions towards a client-based approach is a direct result of purely financial considerations.) According to Bourdieu, it is the many "techniques of rational domination that impose over-involvement in work (and not only among management) and work under emergency or high-stress conditions" (1998, 3).

Many believed that critical reason, cost efficiency, and techno-science would allow the the human race to enter a better age, freed from illusions. Rationality would give us what we desired—the ability to reach our optimal level of accomplishment. In "Les nouveaux maîtres du monde" ("The World's New Masters"), Ignacio Ramonet focused on this singular habit of thought, which by definition excludes all human considerations: concentrate all power into the hands of a few financiers, whose only aim is to increase profits (1995, 2). This way of thinking is, however, increasingly losing the charmed quality that modernity promised.

Today, numerous signs indicate that this economic paradigm, which governs our professional and personal lives, is weakening. John Kenneth Galbraith, in his *Economics in Perspective* (1987), calls attention to the important ideological slippage brought about by economics. This sector of human activity has opted to focus on calculations, cash flow, and economic transactions instead of pursuing ethical questioning around issues such as poverty, exploitation,

la concurrence entre filiales autonomes, entre équipes contraintes à la polyvalence et, enfin, entre individus, à travers l'individualisation de la relation salariale": "L'essence du néolibéralisme," Le Monde diplomatique (March 1998); http://www.mondediplomatique.fr/1998/03/bourdieu/10167.

and power relationships. It is because these concerns have been pushed into the background that we now see an increase in social demands and a return to questions of ethics. Some, among them Peter Berger (1999), use the term *desecularization* when talking about the process that has been set in motion.

This desecularization is carried forward mainly by small groups or civil associations. Their demands are based on the need to respect the environment, on the increasing disparity between rich and poor, on problems of exclusion, intolerance, discrimination, and iniquity—in short, on the enduring forms of social injustice that prevent us from achieving social harmony. These issues call for a profound change in the way leadership operates.

It is not surprising to note the rising demands for social justice from groups opposing neoliberal organizations and governments that have divorced themselves from all social responsibility and promote instead the current imperatives of a market economy to justify their actions. The modernization of the state, grafted onto the liberalization of markets, raises questions about leadership that remain little discussed.

Most of the time, the strategic arsenal that is put in place is intended to guide management according to a specific model. For now, this is a management of instrumental rationality that offers a single-minded vision: profitability and productivity. Within these confines, individuals are left with little room to manoeuvre, as most choices are imposed by the company. The exercise of power seems to be motivated exclusively by the desire for productivity, triumphantly announcing the dawn of a new era, in which greater flexibility in working conditions and heightened worker autonomy will be the rule.

This conviction is, however, devoid of any real human or social foundation and is nothing more than the rhetoric of the new public management (NPM), which claims to want to de-bureaucratize organizations and improve life at work. In fact, this rhetoric is meant to divert attention from the real issues. The choices made have major repercussions on workers, who are given less and less scope for self-determination and find themselves helpless in the face of a cumbersome administrative bureaucracy and the need to adhere strictly to official procedures. In such a context, how can they exercise their capacity for judgment and reflection? This situation rather forces them to subscribe to a sort of "ready-to-wear" thinking, easily disposable, that leads to shortcuts in terms of conscientiousness and most always to a short-term vision.

This orientation is not without its impact on those who find themselves in positions of authority, as well as on those who are subject to their authority. Naturally, these circumstances generate tensions, but they also create paradoxes, the meaning of which is increasingly elusive to those who confront them on a daily basis. The effects of this trend are perverse: constraints on the expression of individualistic attitudes at work, the cult of performance, and a heightened degree of standardization that is more and more the norm (Lipovetsky 1983). This ideology naturally has its effect on the behaviour and values of people. We observed the predominance of a certain relativism, the loss of a sense of shared standards, the precariousness of moral values, and a sort of alienation of moral judgment.

Another perverse effect is linked to the excessive use of legal recourse, which justifies and protects anything, even incompetence. How many times have we heard of managers grappling with incompetent employees who are protected by corporate interests, to the detriment of the common good? As Jacques Grand'Maison (1999) rightly points out, our relations with others are increasingly legalistic. Our ability to analyze has been handed over almost exclusively to making procedural and strategic judgments. We do not wish to contest such judgments, because they are necessary, and they have lead to significant advances. However, when used to excess, they lead to distortions, misinterpretation, and friction in the workplace that are increasingly difficult to resolve. This legalistic way of thinking has altered normal relations with others. The only relationship available is one based on force rather than on dialogue. In the face of this narrow conception of human interaction, the social bond gradually decays, culminating in a kind of Gordian knot, sometimes impossible to undo.

Another recent trend, towards increased departmentalization, is also evident in many organizations. Each sphere of activity has become autonomous, thereby reducing knowledge to a fragmented, compartmentalized vision. A mechanistic separation has set in, which stifles creativity that otherwise might result in some sort of synchronism (see Senge et al. 2004). When forging basic links is a challenge, it is not surprising how difficult it becomes to create frames of reference within which individuals can recognize their place.

This way of thinking can be applied only with difficulty to social systems, as it leads us to perceive problems, and reality itself, in a fragmented manner, which again constitutes paradox. Indeed, living systems are not a collection of various parts; rather, they change, grow, and adapt as a whole, at once coherent and incoherent, but essentially organic. This organic reality contradicts a mechanistic vision, such as that outlined by Gareth Morgan in his book on organizational metaphors, *Images of Organization* (1997). Our social relationships continuously evolve in the course of our contact with other people during our daily lives. Human beings are always engaged in creating new structures—interdependencies—in a constant flux.

The Uneasy Overlap Between Modernism and Postmodernism

As noted earlier, the vision offered by positivism and carried over by modernity has resulted in a rationality detached from values, which clouds "mathematical" judgment and complicates the decision-making process. A split exists between our two worlds—the Cartesian world, which grew out of science and came to flower in the modern era, and a world in the process of *re-enchantment*, which is rooted in concepts that allow room for the interdisciplinarity of postmodernism. Philosophy describes postmodernity as a passage into another age that engages critique of the previous period, namely modernity. The representatives of the postmodern trend, such as Jürgen Habermas and Jean-François Lyotard, speak of modified boundaries and knowledge. According to Lyotard, in this postmodern condition, knowledge is not merely the instrument of power; it refines our sensibility to difference and strengthens our ability to bear the incommensurable (1984, 9). All the same, this passage from one era to the next is marked by an incessant back and forth motion between a reassuring vision of the past and an uncertain future. For some, these developments are a feature of the postmodern era, while for others they represent a sort of radicalization of modernity. Indeed, this radicalization comes about when certain concepts that are vectors of modernity—such as critical reason and individualism—undergo rapid expansion. Radicalization, in turn, seems to create a rupture of the sort that makes people receptive to such dimensions as spirituality, ethics, and values.

In Search of an Authentic Rationality

The first factor that can create confusion in terms of people's judgment is the conception of reality that currently prevails in the decision-making process. Rationality, as we know it, was developed around a material vision. It reflects perspectives that are often one-dimensional, fragmented, and divided, which seems to us to drift away from reality because it does not represent the very nature of what rationality should be. We are not calling rationality into question, because it is necessary, but rather the form it currently assumes, in which rationality is seen from the point of view of instrumental reason. Charles Taylor tells us that instrumental reason is that "rationality which we use when we evaluate the simplest means of arriving at a final purpose. Maximum efficiency, the greatest productivity, measures its success" (1992, 15). This vision must be refreshed by taking the moral dimension into account. The points made by Édgar Morin and Anne Brigitte Kern offer us an interesting lead concerning this redefinition, in line with a postmodern vision:

True rationality is by nature open and engaged in dialogue with the real, which resists it. It constantly goes back and forth between the logical instance and the empirical instance; it is the fruit of debate of ideas, and not the property of a system of ideas.

. . .

True rationality can be recognized by its capacity to recognize its own shortcomings. (1993, 188, 192)

Rationality, so described, brings to light a dialectical process that is detached from all ideological reference and games of influence. The nature of rationality rests not in deliberation or negotiation but rather in dialogue. The latter is an important concept in terms of moral theories, involving, as it does, concern for others. Likewise, it expresses an appreciation for the distinctiveness of each person. Dialogue does not radicalize social relationships; it is an invitation to openness and the conservation of this social bond. In this way, we see the burgeoning of an inclusive sensibility characterized by dialogue and the recognition of complexity.

Dialogue Versus Deliberation

The practice of dialogue—a term often used by international organizations, such as UNESCO or the United Nations—is distinct from a more deliberative model in which only those who possess a well-developed power of argument succeed in making their point of view understood. The argumentative model, so prevalent in law and politics, is clearly encouraged in Western societies. Applied to leadership, it would be known as leadership by influence. Feminist philosophers have criticized this argumentative, deliberative model as one that silences too many voices (Gendron 2003; Young 1996; Jaggar 1995; Noddings 1984). According to Iris Young, the "tendency to restrict democratic discussion to argument carries implicit cultural biases that can lead to exclusions in practice" (1996, 122). As Claude Gendron points out:

[The deliberative model] emphasizes the use of reason instead of political power, each person having an equal vote, regardless of his social position or power. The process is based on argument, and only the force of the best argument is accepted as a suitable element to guide the participants to a mutual agreement. However, the rational nature of this agreement requires that there be equality between participants in the debate, and that each is able to express himself freely in a forum free from domination. (2003, 59)[6]

The question is, how does one know which is the *best argument*? By its power of persuasion, or its influence, or its popularity, or by some other criterion? According to Young, this "forum free from domination" proves difficult to create. The search for a different, inclusive mode of communication responds to a need that clearly exists in the hierarchical workplace. For instance, during the 60th Congress on Ethics and Dilemmas Within Organizations, in 2005, a number of participants, from various government agencies, trade unions, and private organizations, indicated the need for dialogue-driven discussion sessions where people could come together to reflect on and identify new solutions to complex challenges. This request is in line with two problems manifest in the workplace: the prevalence of individualistic behaviour, one the one hand, and the need to strengthen collective relationships, on the other. This ongoing tug of war is but one of the challenges faced by organizations.

By way of example, let us look at some research carried out in a hospital environment on absenteeism and the organization of labour, which offers some insight into the process of dialogue. This project, carried out in 2006 and 2007, aimed to create an

---

6. In the original: "privilégie l'emploi de la raison en lieu et place du pouvoir politique, chaque personne dispose d'une voix équivalente, indépendamment de sa position sociale ou de pouvoir. Le processus repose sur l'argumentation, et seule la force du meilleur argument est retenue comme élément approprié pour guider les participants vers un commun accord. Le caractère rationnel de cet accord exige toutefois qu'il y ait égalité entre les personnes participant au débat, que chacun et chacune puisse s'exprimer librement dans un espace de parole exempt de domination."

understanding of the phenomenon of absenteeism at work (Langlois and Marcoux 2007). The hospital administrators were very concerned about the problem of absenteeism, which was significantly affecting organizational efficiency. At an initial meeting, it was agreed to invite various targeted staff—nurses, nursing auxiliaries, managers, executives, physicians—to engage in a dialogue-driven discussion with the goal of identifying the causes of absenteeism and determining its impact on the organization. When the discussion process was elaborated, several members of the management team—which included general management, financial management, human resources, and advisors—voiced their concern about the composition of such a group and its capacity for exchange: to gather different groups of employees together was not a common practice. We quickly noticed that the group was divided between those who adhered to a fragmented notion of roles and those who thought in terms of existing social relationships and who saw the possibility of moving beyond "roles" in order to negotiate a workable solution. This tension notwithstanding, we noticed that the logic that prevailed and that produced a degree of consensus was that anchored in a technical and instrumental rationality. The concept of social relationships had to remain subordinate to this logic. Eventually, management agreed to give it a try. After six months during which a trial organization was put in place, one that relied on dialogue, the experience proved to be very meaningful for everyone involved. One of the major gains was an enhanced understanding of the work that each person does and the impact it has on the work that others do. Everyone felt a sense of solidarity and interdependence, which was due mainly to the discussion groups set up in the workplace. Several people realized that meeting as a team, a practice that had existed previously but had been abandoned, needed to be reinstated for the good of all.

This study of an approach based on discussion and the establishment of inclusive dialogue groups showed that these definitely met a need. Nevertheless, the project of establishing dialogue must overcome a major obstacle when put into practice: the habit of seeing efficiency exclusively in terms of supposed savings of time. Dialogue is often considered a "waste of time," but this does not correspond to the actual profile of productivity.

Individualism: The Construction of Personal Meaning

Another typically postmodern phenomenon is the rise of individualism. No doubt the recognition of individual rights has had positive ramifications in terms of a recognition of personhood. This trend was formalized with the recognition of human rights, with its implied values of respect, dignity, and consideration for the person. The concept of human rights also allowed individuals to become emancipated and to distance themselves from holism—a social concept in which personal sovereignty is voluntarily limited in the interests of the whole. Over the years, the notion of personal fulfillment has become a fixture in our daily lives. As François de Singly (2005) notes, individualism currently gets bad press, as it is often associated with the tyranny of the free market, with the survival of the fittest, with indifference to others, with egocentrism, and with incivility. Even while many of the ills of postmodern society are attributed to individualism, the fact remains that it calls into question the very foundations of our way of living together, a cohabitation that is constantly being redefined. For organizations, this trend presents a great challenge, especially in the context of the better management of human resources in an organization that is trying, for better or for worse, to mobilize its employees.

The tendency to keep others at a distance can reveal an underlying sense of powerlessness. It also suggests that people are having difficulty in agreeing on common terms of reference. In the past, religions played a guiding role by imposing certain collective norms, but these were often exclusive and established without the necessary links to other religious groups. This brought about a form of ostracism, the fallout from which is still abundantly evident. Frédéric Lenoir (2005) notes that people today take their bearings from here and there, despite a lack of coherence among these various points of reference and without establishing links between them, which results in a sort of autonomization of the subject. Some also see therein a sort of relativism, a religion à la carte or ad hoc ethics.

This diversity of meaning and values is an increasingly important issue. It has destabilized our relationships and our professional behaviour because it includes so many challenges to social consensus and matters of collective living. One of these challenges consists of the proposal that we insist on tolerant behaviour, which many see as moral relativism. Such tolerance can, in theory, allow individuals who hold different beliefs to coexist in an organization. However, in practice, tolerance imposes certain limits on the search for genuine understanding, such as dialogue demands. Tolerance is not total indifference, but neither is it a positive act of respect. As Mirabeau declared in 1789, tolerance is insufficient. We must go beyond this stage and strive instead for mutual understanding. It is very clear that the imperative of autonomy has become a daily way of life, but this imperative can collide with anything that commands obedience, control, or conformity. The refusal to enter into a logic of obedience without asking questions is one of the characteristics of individualism, which, in the context of the workplace, challenges the working contract, whether written or unwritten, demanding that it take into account this need for autonomy. Those concerned point to the voluntary character of compliance, to the mutual agreement that is necessary to the success of an undertaking that requires some level of personal engagement. During our research at the hospital, we were surprised to discover the extent to which people seeking to improve the way work was organized had to confront resistance on the part of co-workers when it came to working collectively. Those involved in such efforts were considered, at best, to be wasting their time and, at worst, were even perceived as traitors.

Through the process of individualization, people create their own frameworks for meaning and are free to choose whether to ascribe to a specific belief. They are able to exercise free will, even if this can be difficult in the face of power games, lobbying, and conflict among competing ideologies. Charles Taylor speaks of the moral ideal, which should be implicit in the process of self-fulfillment, as being a form of truth in itself (1992, 28). But this inevitably introduces a certain complexity into collective relationships that concern our behaviour in the workplace.

Collective Relations in Need of Reconstruction

Another phenomenon that characterizes the transition between the modern and postmodern periods is the way in which we live out our collective relations. The influence of Adam Smith cannot be overlooked in this regard. In *The Theory of Moral Sentiments* (1759), he concretized the way in which we view relations with others. In developing a model that promoted an ethics of interests founded on a particular vision of economics, Smith stated very clearly that every person must pursue self-interest in order for society to function. It is in this manner alone that society will realize its collective interests and, in the process, arrive at a condition of happiness (Gunn 1989). Or, as Jacques Godbout put it in 1993, the production of goods has prevailed over the quality of bonds, a phenomenon characteristic of contemporary society.

Today's problems—environmental degradation, a declining sense of belonging, social disintegration—raise the question of moral obligation and duty. Solutions to these problems depend on our capacity to question ourselves about who we are and what kind of society we want, about what we are doing and the reasons that drive us to do it—in short, about our capacity to become involved and to call ourselves to account for our actions without resorting to avoidance or retreat. Calling ourselves to account does not distance us from others. On the contrary, this behaviour helps us to stay connected to reality and thus to witness the repercussions our actions can have if we carry them out in a relational framework.

This capacity for connection that verges on an ethics of reliance, such as that described by Édgar Morin (2005), does not deny the grey areas, nor the fact that we cannot explain everything, that there exists a sort of indeterminacy, and that, despite this lack of precision, we can rely on our capacity to become involved. We develop relationships and involve ourselves therein, because, in the course of our involvement, we form bonds to others. This is the way life is. We do not live by explanations alone; rather, we live because of our participation in the encounters we have in the course of random activities. This way of being reduces the distance between ourselves and others.

Our participation in these encounters constitutes a challenge when it comes to the construction of our collective relationships, inasmuch as we live in relation with others. It seems increasingly difficult to close one's eyes to the consequences of our actions and the impact these have on others. As George Wald observes, "The past few years have made us aware, as never before, of the depth of kinship among all living organisms. . . . So all life is akin, and our kinship is much closer than we had ever imagined" (1996, 46).

Accordingly, we must abandon the vision that affords primacy to instrumental reason in order to break open the *iron cage* spoken of by Max Weber. For Charles Taylor, it is possible for us to free ourselves from this cage by "deliberating what ought to be our ends, and whether instrumental reason ought to play a lesser role in our lives than it does" (1992, 19). Taylor underscores that instrumental reason yields only a limited range of choices, restricting us to a narrow vision, and makes us see reality as if it were a tunnel, or the circular model of intelligence advanced by Plato. According to Taylor, institutions and structures founded on techno-industrial reason "force individuals to accord these a weight we would never otherwise offer them in a serious moral debate and which could prove to be extremely destructive" (1992, 20). Instrumental reason finds itself powerfully shaken when it is questioned by the new ethical issues raised, especially, by technological and biological developments.

Individualism and the search for new collective relationships constitute one of the issues of the postmodern period. The challenge is to rethink our behaviour in the light of new standards of acceptability while allowing ourselves space for dialogue. When discussion revolves around what we consider acceptable or not, we are able to get beyond the famous *politically correct* as soon as we reconsider our choices, our institutions, and the way in which we function. Unfortunately, this process sometimes leads to another extreme: the desire to make everything *ethically correct*. This orientation ensures that our reflective capacity in relation to ethics finds itself outbidded by a normative approach that borrows its logic exclusively from a misuse of legal technique, an effect also seen in the use of *ethical codes*.

This restrictive legal logic forces us to choose between the tolerable, that is, behaviour deemed permissible by law and rules, and the intolerable, or conduct that society does not condone. Given such logic, it is difficult to reflect on what might be the best decision to make. What is considered tolerable does not necessarily encompass everything there is in terms of the social good. It is by questioning this that we create an ethical space, one that can lend coherence to human actions, a space in which it is possible to reflect on outcomes and on the actions to be undertaken. As such, consequences come to determine what is ethical.

To open oneself to ethical reasoning requires that we take more time to reflect on what constitutes ideal behaviour. In collective relations, the accent is on ultimate ends and shared values.

Social Regulations: What Regulations?

One question that often arises during exchanges with ethicists concerns the view of ethics solely as a mode of social regulation (Boisvert et al. 2003). Ethics proposes social regulations of its own, but this is not its only function. What type(s) of regulation would be necessary to sustain an ethical practice? Philosophers, like ethicists, apply an autoregulatory mode to ethics. The autonomy of the subject is paramount in initiating ethical reflection on various issues or in the case of a moral dilemma. Making a decision relieves the individual (free agent and accountable for his actions), but the search for the path to follow can and often must be carried out with others, and this to the benefit of all. Moreover, the exercise of reflection must be added to this, that which provokes reconsideration. The resulting decision will be confronted by heteroregulatory modes. Institutionally speaking, the individual is not a disembodied being. He is faced with labour standards, laws, organizational policies, and regulations. He cannot ignore this universe with which he is called to comply. However, through ethical reflection, nothing can stop him from questioning certain practices or regulations that might seem inappropriate in a given context.

We believe that in order for ethics to be fully actualized in daily life, it is imperative to have a thoughtful mix of these two modes of regulation: autoregulation and heteroregulation. Sometimes, a hybrid mode will be necessary, whence the importance of a rebalancing exercise with regard to these modes of regulation, in accordance with critical thinking.

Ethical Demands

The quest for ethics is situated in the context described above. New requirements, with which workers are burdened, have put great pressure on them in terms of decisions they must make. This generates a certain complexity, which in turn makes it necessary to reflect deeply on the issues and the imaginable consequences. It is essential to understand this ethical quest fully. Where does it come from? What makes it so popular today?

According to some authors (Legault 1999; Bourgeault 2004), the need for ethics became apparent in the wake of recent major financial scandals as well as advances in bioethics and stem-cell research. According to Frédéric Lenoir (2005), we are experiencing a radicalization of modernity, bearing in mind that certain defining concepts of the modern period—critical reason and individualism—have been subject to an intensification, thereby provoking this radicalization. The latter ensures that people are ready to open themselves up to dimensions that touch on spirituality, ethics, and values. Generally, one notices that receptivity to the axiological dimension is present at the organizational level. A certain primacy is attributed to values such as integrity, transparency, and equity, at least in organizational discourse.[7] We believe that the challenge lies in action, but we will return to this in the presentation of our TERA model.

This shift towards practices that emphasize the importance of values to an organization can take a variety of forms. One of these seeks to provide organizations with codes of conduct designed to put an end to behaviour that could seem deviant or to offer standard procedures for conflict resolution. The manner in which these codes are developed is crucial and shows once again that logic is privileged. Here, the danger lies in developing a code of conduct based on the logic of instrumental rationality while pursuing outcomes that are often anchored in dialogical rationality. What is the legitimacy of these codes? Is such a code also binding on its authors? And how can ethics be imposed by authority? Are we faced with a postmodern way of imposing a professional code on wage earners? No doubt, the way such codes are constructed will reveal either an *imposed* approach or one that invites fully conscious and voluntary support. The latter is much closer to an ethical organizational approach. Table 2 highlights the two prevailing models in organizations in terms of codes of conduct or the articulation of values.

I observed that in organizations that follow an ethical path, instrumental logic and the logic of dialogue tend to overlap, sometimes producing a certain confusion. We are witnessing a kind of fragmentation of these two modes of logic, which can generate numerous contradictions. Constructing an approach based on a code of behaviour, or on a statement of values, or on specific ethical strategies—these do not promote the same ethical aim. What is often heard is that organizations want responsible and autonomous employees while at the same time they confine them within an instrumental logic that can stifle critical reflection and prevent the exercise of judgment. The human capacity that an ethical orientation engenders strives to go beyond an exclusive normality and beyond the inappropriate use of legal methods.

---

7. On the concept of integrity, see Brown 2005.

Table 2: Two Modes of Rationality in Developing Organizational Goals

	INSTRUMENTAL RATIONALITY	DIALOGICAL RATIONALITY
Conception	Conceived by a small, often homogenous group or by external consultants (top-down)	Conceived by a heterogeneous group that is representative of the organization (bottom-up)
Regulatory mode	Heteroregulatory	Autoregulatory, forming part of a shared process of elaboration
Conduct	Modelling (of behaviour)	Consciousness raising (raising ethical sensitivity) and authenticity
Power	Sanction	Empowerment
Environment	Adaptation	Recognition of the real and its complexity
Decision	Standardization and conformity	Result of a shared reflective process
Outcome	Socialization	Transformation (that has meaning for individuals)

The first part of this book has highlighted assumptions related to the two visions—the modern and the postmodern—that now intermingle in organizations and influence our behaviour at work and our way of perceiving the real. This discussion did not aim to create an exhaustive list of elements that make up these currents of thought but rather to focus attention on the construction of a form of rationality that has now advanced to the point that it prevents us from seeing the real.

The interest in ethical and in axiological considerations developed simultaneously as a reaction to the capitalist market economy. The two ways of perceiving and understanding reality have progressed in parallel, without crossing each other. However, one cannot but notice that the merchant model is tending to come apart and is showing signs of losing impetus, which leads us to reposition ethical reflection and re-examine the values implicit in our organizations. In this respect, the events of 11 September 2001 reopened discussions on universal values and the need for reflection on the position these occupy. Is there room to situate these values outside the Western straitjacket in which traditional references have become even more precarious following these dramatic events? There is no doubt that the debate on universal values is nothing new.

Today, there is a forceful return to ethical reflection, with questions raised about the goals being pursued. This is a serious challenge, because it is not easy to find consensus on what is considered part of ethics. Neither is it easy to revisit the concept without producing tension between what is legitimate and acceptable and what Ricoeur (2004) so beautifully calls an "intertwining of lights" ("entrecroiser des lumières"),[8] which can serve to clarify approaches far removed from morality and ideology. This clarification, distinct from ideology, gives back a privileged place to discernment and free will in order to question what is normative and to put ethics at the service of social justice.

The second part of this book deals with ethics as a decision-making mode. We will define this concept in light of advances in the areas of moral theory, of educational administration, and of management, and we will present a process of ethical decision making that aims to be responsible and authentic, one that can be discerned among those who practice ethical leadership.

---

8. For the French original, see Ricoeur, "Projet universel et multiplicité des héritages," in *Où vont les valeurs? Entretiens de XXIe siècle*, ed. Jérôme Bindé (Paris: Éditions de UNESCO/Albin Michel, 2004)

CHAPTER 2

Ethical Leadership
The Anglo-Saxon Understanding

THE OVERALL OBJECTIVE OF THIS chapter is to address the concept of ethical decision making in leaders who are striving to be ethical, especially managers of educational institutions, which was the area of my research for more than a decade. I intend to bring to light the ethical nature of the decision-making component of leadership and to root its meaning in theory. I do not wish to re-examine these theories in detail, as numerous authors have already dealt with these subjects, and their books, which judiciously retrace the evolution of these concepts, can serve as a reference. I am interested instead in examining the daily exercise of such leadership.

Following a brief theoretical overview, I will move on to the concrete part of this book, namely the development of an ethical decision-making process for use in the workplace. My concept of ethical leadership seen through a decision-making process is in line with the work of Peter Senge, which deals with systematic learning (Senge 2005; Senge and Gauthier 1991). I chose this perspective because I believe it is possible to develop a greater ethical conscience, both at the individual and organizational levels, and to learn about ethics at work.

I set out from the premise that ethical leadership can help lead to greater synchronicity in collective workplace training. Why associate the concept of ethical leadership with the theory of learning organizations? In the course of the TERA research project,[1] I noticed that learning about ethics was easier when individuals had developed a veritable learning organization, in line with that advanced by Senge. The establishment of a learning organization promotes the ties and the confidence necessary to grapple with ethics at work because it starts out as co-elaboration of meaning, lending it moral legitimacy.

The vision I am proposing for ethical leadership is that it must not devolve upon a single individual but should rather be a collective responsibility, that of developing a structure that favours autonomy for all players seeking to improve the way they carry out their work and, by so doing, offering a responsible and global approach to efficiency. The association of my concept of ethical leadership with this theory allows us to exercise within an institution not a leadership in the true sense of the word but rather a fundamental principle of questioning what is essential in organizations. Before addressing this aspect more fully, however, I will define what I understand ethics to mean.

The Concept of Ethics

As Paul Ricoeur (1992) did, I use the words *ethical* and *moral* interchangeably, as they both refer to mores, or conduct. Their etymological roots are different, but it is possible to afford them both the same practical meaning. The word *ethics* comes from the Greek *ethos*, while the word *moral* derives from the Latin *mores*. There is no clearly accepted definition for ethics. I believe that ethics shows us what it is best to do. The concept is defined either by a reflexive process relating to the notion of what is good or by a collection of

1. The TERA research project, titled Vers un Trajectoire éthique, responsable et authentique (Towards an Ethical, Responsible, and Authentic Trajectory), was subsidized by a grant from the Social Sciences and Humanities Research Council of Canada (2005–2008).

normative rules. Ethics overlaps these two dimensions, because it is at once internal and external; it is endogenous. It enlists the process of reflection in order to distance the subject from what is happening. This stepping back allows us to identify, among other things, norms, values, and conclusions by anticipating the possible consequences of a decision. Such choices are those of a responsible person, one who is conscious of his or her actions and their consequences and who is capable of taking responsibility for them. This work of reflection serves as armour for judgment. This relationship with ethics is part of a search for much greater degree of consciousness and capacity for reflection, which can actually become a major challenge in organizations that favour speed and the capacity to react rapidly to situations.

Ethics as a reflexive capacity is not a panacea. However, it does emphasize the importance of the exercise of free will and the moral evaluation of consequences, and it allows for the keen exercise of discernment and judgment.

Monique Canto-Sperber points out that reflection abides by rules and principles according to which we develop our beliefs; it allows us to understand the reasons for these beliefs and to recognize within these a normative impact (2001, 236). This work of reflection cannot pretend to be objective because it originates with our own point of view. Hannah Arendt states that imagination supports the work of reflection, in that it allows one to look from nowhere to oneself, to be a spectator of the world, to be one's own actor, to achieve some distance by journeying to the interior space of others (see Canto-Sperber 2001, 236–237).[2] Therefore, if we are unable to claim complete objectivity, what is left in terms of our reflective capacity would be, in my opinion, our level of conscience or moral sensitivity. This pertains both to moral theories and to the area of ethics, more specifically, to applied ethics. I will explore

---

2. Arendt develops her ideas in *Lectures on Kant's Political Philosophy* (Chicago: University of Chicago Press, 1992) and in *Responsibility and Judgment*, ed. Jerome Kohn (New York: Schocken Books, 2003). See also Ronald Beiner and Jennifer Nedelsky, eds., *Judgment, Imagination, and Politics: Themes from Kant and Arendt* (Lanham, MD: Rowman & Littlefield, 2001).

this important component further in the section on ethical decision making.

The cultural dimension is also important in this process of reflection because, quite apart from the fact that culture reflects what is normal, what is acceptable, and what is legitimate in society, it contributes to lending specificity to ethics without depriving it of its distancing effect. This precision ensures that ethics has an active social context, from which it draws its dynamic character. Ethics is therefore a reflection that precedes action: it attempts to understand how the logic of action has been woven, what legitimates it, and what its ultimate goals may be. Ethics is reflection under construction,[3] because it is built bit by bit, with the help of other points of view. Seen in this manner, ethics can be regarded as the heart of leadership.

Ethical Leadership

Ethics cannot be considered a management tool, because it is hereby that individuals rise to the peak of our organizations.

—Marc Leclerc, CEGEP deputy director, St-Hyacinthe

In the world today, it is increasingly difficult to lead with a clear vision of reality. Situations are complex, the context changes rapidly; obligations and duties are rarely fully defined and well delimited. More and more, rights are demanded without thought for their accompanying obligations and without taking into consideration the issue of accountability, whose indicators do not always fit with organizational realities. To this is added an understanding and application of variable geometric norms. For some, applying a standard or rule can become unethical because each situation demands analysis, rather than a blanket solution. Standards thus represent an obstacle to ethical action. For others, rules must be applied without necessarily requiring any critical reflection because their purpose is

---

3. "Une réflexion en chantier," an expression that was used by Guy Paquet during the 2005 Congress on Ethics and Dilemmas Within Organizations and one that we find very representative of ethics in metaphorical terms.

to assist in quick decision making. A good conscience has thus been preserved since the rules have been respected. However, the good conscience of some is not always the good conscience of others. In such a context, making an ethical decision can become a perilous obstacle course through a maze of reflection and organizational rules. The path is fraught with pitfalls and may require a certain moral fortitude. This dimension is little discussed in either the literature on administration and management or in university circles. However, when talking to managers, they are unanimous in their affirmation that making decisions today requires a certain amount of courage. People face new human, organizational, or structural challenges and thus encounter increasing difficulty when depending on their moral and professional capacities to identify solutions that go beyond the simple status quo. The complexity, the movement, the pressure, and the abundance of information combine to shape the administrative landscape. This raises numerous questions about the way organizations are currently led.

This different approach to leadership demands adopting new professional standards of conduct at work, from the promotion of more high-minded attitudes to the search for values that have the power to unite. All these elements are often regarded as ideals, which can seem utopian to some. However, many people, workers and leaders alike, have a profound desire to bring about sustainable, more human change in the workplace. This path leads towards ethical leadership.

Nurturing New Social Relationships

Being a real leader does not mean wanting to be popular; rather, it means attempting to make decisions that are good for one's organization.

—Anne McGee, secondary school principal, Ontario

Given these premises, I believe that a profound reappraisal of the concept of leadership is necessary. Indeed, one finds that the

35

literature on leadership offers a list of the characteristics of those who serve in important positions that one can supposedly emulate. When potential leaders, armed with their diplomas, go for an interview, they are subjected to a battery of tests meant to assess their style of leadership. This very technical approach, however, does not reveal how such qualities might be destabilized in a real working environment. Some who work in human resources do not hesitate to transcend such technical preoccupations. Leadership style and job title are of no use in resolving situations that involve substantial ethical dilemmas, where black and white blend into grey. The sense of authority needed to handle complex situations does not automatically come with leadership, as these two terms are not synonymous. Being in a position of authority means having a defined institutional role in which certain modes of behaviour, attitudes, and actions prevail. It is in the context of these social relationships that ethical leadership becomes manifest. As abundant research has shown (see, for example, Brunet and Savoie 2003), a leader does not necessarily have a well-defined institutional role in the organization. My work focused on men and women in positions of authority who manifested a certain form of leadership. The question that those in situations of authority should ask themselves is whether they are exercising ethical leadership. Is this a moral obligation they must take on? I believe that these simple questions are part of an important shift that is only now beginning to occur in institutions and businesses.

This focus placed on the role, the personality traits, and the behavioural characteristics that one should emulate in order to become a leader, which are sometimes formulated as recipes, stands in contrast to the concept of ethical leadership advanced in these pages. It is surprising to note that the most popular works written on leadership focus on prescriptions for character and behaviour and deal with forms of personal management that recommend investing in one's self as capital for growth (Salamon 2005).

"As stated by linguist Robin Lakoff, works on therapy in the twentieth century are like works on etiquette or propriety in the last century," Arlie Russell Hochschild observed in *The Managed Heart*. "This is because propriety has impregnated emotional life very profoundly" (1983, 192). What is unhealthy in such proposals is explicitly putting forward the personal qualities that one needs in order to be a good leader, which leads to the belief that one is free and autonomous. Furthermore, as de Gaulejac put it: "We trivialize competition as a model of social relations, we transform society into a playground, we trivialize the megalomaniac quest of our leaders and consider as natural the idea of economic warfare. When everyone wants to be a champion, no one is any longer preoccupied with the common good" (2005, 137).

For Bill George, leaders are defined for the most part by their values and characters (2003, 20), and, we would add, the whole is concretized in social relations with others. These qualities seem to play an important part today. Peter Northouse (2004) highlights three skills essential to the practice of true leadership, namely, problem solving, exercising judgment, and understanding. When I examined these three skills, I noted that they have their own meaning with regard to ethical leadership. Problem solving has become complex and requires more than a legal and administrative mode of interrogation, as such an approach, which is exclusively normative, reveals significant gaps in terms of proposed solutions. Judgment is a capacity that lies at the heart of ethics, a capacity that must be exercised with due rigour (Canto-Sperber 2001). This faculty will play an essential role in today's context, as people are called upon to clarify the circumstances under which judgment is exercised, something that brings with it a certain responsibility, both moral and social. As Richard Sennett observes:

An authority figure is someone who assumes responsibility for the power he exercises. . . . Modern techniques of management attempt to escape to the authoritarian side of such declarations by trying at the same time not to be held accountable for their actions. . . . If the responsible agent is none other than "change," and the whole world is a "victim," the authority disappears because no one is any longer responsible, especially the leader who lets people leave. It is the pressures of the market that are expected to carry out his work. (2000, 161)

The context becomes the justification that explains both everything and nothing. It has as its pretext to diminish or channel the responsibility that devolves upon persons in positions of authority. Faced with this fact, people struggle with calling into question the meaning and consequences of their decisions (or, sometimes, their indecision). Most of the time, this is accompanied by an attitude from which emotion is absent.

In terms of ethics, moral responsibility demands that a person become responsible. Moral responsibility also rests on one's ability to manage oneself, to be active, to take charge of oneself—in short, to be the subject of one's actions. But as someone told me during my research, "one cannot be accountable for everything." According to Alain Ehrenberg, "to the extent that the demand for autonomy permeates the whole of social life, both private and public, the tendency for each to be responsible for all asserts itself as the authority of a rule, and this regardless of its proper place in the social hierarchy" (2005, 37). What we have here is a paradox, one produced by the demand for greater responsibility and the demand for greater autonomy. How do we explain this tension? I believe that the meaning of responsibility gets lost in the administrative maze: it is increasingly difficult to know who does what and who is responsible for what. Furthermore, the demand for autonomy is not understood in its true sense, namely, that of a greater accountability for actions we carry out freely. Instead, autonomy is generally conceived and practiced in an individualistic manner that often ignores others and is rather embedded in egocentric relationships. By asking people to be autonomous, one is requiring them to manage themselves according to well-defined limits in line with their own will.

For example, autonomy with regard to decisions is an important element in the exercise of authority. But are individuals able to exercise this authority, or are they subject to heterogenous demands, in which criteria are set down without leaving individuals a genuine margin of manoeuvrability, one that would allow for transforming situations for the better? According to Christian Maroy:

> Conceded decision-making autonomy is never related only to operational decisions, decisions to adapt to uncertainties and unforeseen hazards within the framework of decisions made by the management staff or the strategic head of the organization without upper-level decisions being challenged. . . . In short, the autonomy offered and encouraged is always managed, delimited, and bound, often so as to make it impossible to turn to more important decisions. (1997, 117)

In such a context, it might seem difficult for some people to practice ethical leadership. Indeed, this concept is not a panacea for resolving all managerial ills. On the contrary, it seeks to place ethical reflection at the heart of leadership action. Faced with this epistemological position, ethical leadership runs along parallel tracks, in that it incorporates numerous elements of the organization while also standing at a distance, which allows challenges to the desired goals to be better seen and understood. The engine of its action differs from leadership in which interests or calculations alone take precedence, because such leadership requires axiological neutrality. This other position, close to the model of a market economy, forces the leader to think otherwise while disconnecting from the "other." According to Charles Taylor, this model must be rejected "in favour of a richer vision, more in keeping with what the human being really is" (1992, 49). To that, we might add that it must also be rejected so that we may develop a greater consciousness regarding our conduct and the decisions we make in the working environment.

Ethical leadership is a first step in this search for a new form of working behaviour. It attempts to distance itself from instrumental relationships in order to promote greater humanization in the workplace through the shared construction of values, which foster commitment. This shared construction of values and goals is vital to ensuring greater coherence in organizations. This commitment, or voice, as some authors call it, is becoming increasingly central: individuals disengage or become disaffected because they no longer feel a sense of personal concern with decisions; they feel they no longer have a place or a voice in their workplace, and this in spite of advances in rights and protections. The phenomenon is as interesting as it is paradoxical: we have a greater degree of protection and more rights but less space in which to discuss sensitive issues that in fact have an impact on people. Everything is organized in relation to representation, in which the group speaks in the name of the interests of its members. But can we ask ourselves what outcomes such interests reflect? This question, if considered carefully, is a first step towards an understanding of the true challenges to ethical leadership. The individual may feel collectively protected but does not feel individually heard.

The Concept of Human Nature

It is interesting to note that, in 1954, Douglas McGregor declared: "Good leadership in industry depends more than any other single thing on the manager's conception of what his job is or of what management is. Second, it depends on his convictions and on his beliefs about people" (32–33). According to McGregor, the "Y" theory, which sees the human being as a responsible person, one who is motivated to work and who favours self-control and autonomous self-direction, represented the modern way, the path to be taken. To this, he later added: "Under proper conditions such results encourage people to direct their creative energies towards organizational objectives, give them some voice in decisions that affect them, and provide significant opportunities for the satisfaction of social and egoistic needs" (1957, 18).

The concept of giving someone a voice in the decision-making process is a *means for satisfying social and egoistic needs*. The goal of giving people a voice, in McGregor's view, is radically different from that advocated by ethical leadership. The concept of the human being implicit in ethical leadership is not as simplistic, and it is much more positive. It rests on the assumption that people are prepared to commit themselves to changing things provided they are given the opportunity in an authentic context. In this sense, the gift theory advanced by Jacques Godbout (2007) can shed light on the human concept advocated by ethical leadership. The author presents several examples of people who, finding themselves in difficult situations (we need only think of the work of Abbé Pierre on behalf of the destitute, associations such as Alcoholics Anonymous, organ donors, and so on), are able to set aside personal interests in order to improve the world around them. When we view human beings as egotists bound up in some sort of moral straightjacket, we lessen the possibility of exploiting their true potential. Such a person is instantly condemned to be perceived in terms of the existing conception, which places a significant restraint on the exercise of leadership itself.

Ethical leadership is a notion that views human nature in a positive way and considers the human being as capable of contributing positively to the development of an organization. Obviously, there will always be people who, for a variety of reasons (physical or psychological illness, unconventional behaviour, lack of competence, incivility, and so on), create greater difficulties at work than others. It is here that responsibility acquires its full meaning by refusing to cover up such behaviour, which, in the end, can poison the work environment. During my research, several people told me about how difficult they found it to react to certain kinds of behaviour, behaviour that, owing to a lack of adequate intervention, only increased and became worse. In order to explain their failure to intervene, people often mentioned the fear of taking action, a lack of audacity, or ignorance. The desire not to displease employees or upset the organization was one of the factors that further served to justify this lack of leadership. Pretending that such behaviour does not exist has significant repercussions in terms of ethical behaviour at work, however. Research on ethics and management is unanimous: a person in a position of authority who trivializes this type of behaviour implicitly accepts such behaviour, thus opening the door to organizational deviance.

Ethical leadership is a concept that is increasingly making its mark on certain areas of administrative science. The concept did not appear all at once but rather emerged by means of a piecemeal analysis of how a manager should act. This rather Kantian dimension (respect for laws, norms, duties, and so on) was brought forward in 1938, when Chester Barnard's *The Functions of the Executive* appeared. Barnard broaches the topic of ethics by mentioning the obligation of the manager to respect the moral sense that exists within an organization and to resolve disputes that arise as this code is applied.

It was only just before the 1980s, however, that we began to see ethics appearing in the literature on management, notably that concerning the structure of the workplace and the conduct appropriate thereto, as part of an analysis of bureaucracy and its perverse effects on human behaviour, with the focus falling on behaviour qualified as unacceptable. For example, Robert Jackall carried out an in-depth analysis of ethos in bureaucracy in "The Moral Ethos of Bureaucracy" (1984) and, some years later, called attention to the lack of ethics among managers in *Moral Mazes: The World of Corporate Managers* (1988). The details that emerged document the distortions of a bureaucracy that, pushed to an extreme, proves to reveal a flagrant lack of ethics. The application of procedures to govern all administrative action, along with the reduction of conscience and behaviour to a set of standards, impede people in their efforts to act and to behave in a responsible manner. Maintaining, at all costs, a culture of management shackled by the dictates of a market economy results in a loss of meaning at work. In such a context, the goal is profit, regardless of the cost and long-term effects on people and the environment. The perverse effect of all this is that, by constantly looking to control behaviour at work, managers curtail the capacities and natural energies of their employees. This approach is, in fact, more about managing *wallets* than about managing people. (In this respect, Max Weber's thoughts on the ethics of conviction offer an incontrovertible starting point. It seems that Weber's stance has not lost any of its topicality when one considers the controversies it sometimes provokes in the field of applied ethics.)

There are currently few published definitions of the concept of ethical leadership. Ethical leadership was first described as a skill needed to guide and inspire people with regard to what is morally right and technically acceptable for the organization (Cuilla 2004; Heifetz 1994). The first empirical works on the subject came from research carried out by Linda K. Treviño (1986). Her work brought to light the ethical characteristics of leaders and the meaning of an ethical culture. This latter concept is closely related to leadership, because it represents values, norms, beliefs, traditions, and common assumptions that guide ethical behaviour. According to Treviño, ethical leadership is vital to the creation of an ethical culture at work. An ethical leader is a leader who cares, who listens to what employees have to say, and who has their best interests in mind. In addition, an ethical leader communicates messages concerning ethics and values, not only during major publicized events but also on a daily basis, through conduct and decisions that reflect a particular ethics. In making decisions, ethical leaders always asks themselves what is best for each employee, for the group, or for the organization as a whole, depending on the situation. Linda Treviño, Michael Brown, and Laura Pincus Hartman (2003) together argue that an ethical leader serves as a model to be emulated in matters of ethics, a model that generates employee confidence and offers an example of the right way to do things in an organization. The ethical leader helps others to become responsible and to define success, not merely in terms of results but also in terms of the way in which one goes about obtaining these results (Treviño 2007).

Authority and Power

The practice of ethical leadership may seem utopian to some. In fact, such leadership sometimes faces an opposition that seems part of the very nature of things: without engaging in an excessive or exclusive quest for gain and power,[4] it aims neither at disproportional control over others nor at gain to the detriment of others. Some doubt that it is possible to put such leadership into place, while other researchers (Brown, Treviño, and Harrison 2005), noting this possibility, have created tools to define such leadership. During my research, I arrived at the same conclusion: that it is possible to develop this leadership by sensitizing people to the different stakes and challenges that make up these practices (Starratt, Langlois, and Duignan 2010).

I am attempting to describe this concept on the basis of my empirical studies. Ethical leadership can be defined as part of a system of actions directed towards raising awareness of conduct in the workplace and towards a search for a common understanding of professional practices. This research requires profound reflection in the course of which values and goals to be pursued are identified. Once this is accomplished, the work of reflection makes up the bedrock on which decisions can be based. Gradually an ethical conscience develops, which leads to a better grasp of reality. This awareness allows for the initiation of critical ethical reflection on a situation, thereby bringing to light the possible choices in terms of potential consequences and long-term effects. Certainly, the reflexive process demands rationality, but this rationality engages in a dialogical relationship that also integrates the transrational mode (moral intuition, and so on) rather than the irrational mode (see Hatcher 2004). The reasons underlying this process exclude *self-interest* and instead aim to improve the practices and quality of the environment by looking for the common good, which rules out a materialistic and calculating spirit.

---

4 Here power can be understood as something other than negative. Ethical leadership exercises power in the service of the common good. In social relations, this is seen as empowerment.

There are other motivations for human action besides purely egotistical interests. The rise of ecological thinking (Dahl 1996; Suzuki 1997) and preoccupations with social concerns offer contemporary examples of other such motivations. Ethical leadership does not belong exclusively to those in authority. Obviously, they are more often able to deploy their ethical actions with greater reach in their organizations. However, every person has the capacity to practice ethical leadership within his or her own sphere of action. Values are at the heart of ethical leadership and are an important vector, alongside authenticity and empowerment. This becomes a fundamental principle by which to examine what is essential in organizations.

Ethics is at the heart of leadership (Ciulla 2004), and the practice of ethical leadership calls for a review of our approach to decision making. In order to understand this position, it proves essential to examine how theories of decision making were fashioned and introduced into the professional environment. I will not attempt to cover all the theories that have been developed but will instead focus on those that have had a positive influence and that predominate in administration and educational management. In so doing, I will talk about theoretical models of ethical decision making.

Decision Making in the Exercise of Leadership

The Theory of Rational Choice

In the first part of this study, we focused on the type of rationality that now prevails and on spin-offs of it that we can observe today. The notion of rationality is often understood in an instrumental mode. For instance, James S. Coleman stated that, according to the theory of rational choices in management, "by acting rationally, a player necessarily commits himself to a process of optimization. One says sometimes that he is maximizing his utility, or that he is minimizing his costs or other" (Coleman and Fararo 1992, xi). When one makes a so-called rational decision, one notices, in light of this theory, that the process of reflection is directed exclusively towards one central factor: the maximization of profits, or greater productivity. This reduces and obscures other dimensions that could help to enrich reflection, such as values, principles, possible consequences, and so on. Furthermore, everything is seen through a lens of quantitative assessment. Admittedly, calculations, algorithms, and statistics are important, but they are only one side of the equation. They do not truly shed light on the meaning and goals pursued, only on one aspect of the situation.

Therefore, the principal course of action is oriented exclusively towards individual interests, where everything is calculated according to axiological neutrality. As Jacques Godbout notes: "The search for one's own interest is the main, not to say the only engine for human action. This is the most extreme position, the harsh version of the theory of rational choice" (2007, 40). The strategic analysis proposed by Michel Crozier and Erhard Friedberg (1977) faces the same challenge in terms of reflexivity. This analysis aims to enhance the power of the actor and his control of the organization and to restore all social relationships to the dimensions of financial interests and capital.

In rational choice theory, instrumental rationality is a rationality of means with respect to the final end. Human action is oriented to a single goal: to make a neutral decision while optimizing results. This rationality is part of linear logic, but it far from reduces uncertainty. As Coleman observes, people are never fully aware of the consequences of their choices, because their judgment excludes important dimensions that would allow them to foresee all possible consequences. From this comes the idea of a certain limited rationality, as advanced by James G. March and Herbert A. Simon (1958).[5]

A Limited Rationality

The works of March and Simon, which deal with an analysis of administrative behaviour as it relates to decisions, have allowed for

---

5. The work of James March and Herbert Simon, as well as that of Richard Cyert and others, constitute what is known as the Carnegie School, which advanced the behavioral theory of the firm.

a highlighting of the concept of limited rationality and the changes experienced within modern organizations. These are part of the domain of cognitive psychology and deal with the analysis of administrative behaviour in relation to decisions. They contest the neoclassical model of rational choice that ignores certain realities: persons who find themselves confronted by limits that prevent them from acting rationally. They bring to light problems relating to the treatment of uncertainty, imperfect information, and the limitations of the calculations of individual agents. For March and Simon, it proves necessary to develop decision-making procedures that focus on processes of training. Simon departs from the scheme that defines rationality as being a method and proposes a model of rationality that serves the investigation of possible choices to be considered in terms of behavioural decisions. Thus, decisional behaviour rests on the selection of possible contingencies, leading to the intervention of potential consequences of decisions linked thereto. Seen in this light, the rationality of decisional behaviour rests on a person's deliberative faculty. According to Simon, rationality denotes a style of behaviour that is appropriate to the realization of given goals and is located within the boundaries imposed by conditions and given constraints (see Favereau 1989). In short, limited rationality, as developed by March and Simon, is made up of cognitive capacities, which are considered relative, and an external environment, marked by complexity. The choices of decision makers rest on "a simplified, limited and rough scheme of the real situation" (March and Simon 1958).

In "From Substantive to Procedural Rationality," Simon broaches the topic of intuitive rationality,[6] which he classifies as a faculty that forms part of limited rationality (1984 [1976]). Intuitive rationality brings to light an approach appropriate for the process of choice: analysis, reasoning, judgment, intuition, and invention. Simon views this faculty as a deliberate and conscious process, which can direct

---

6. Intuition, as viewed by Simon, involves known situations and allows for the selection of elements that have been learned by the subject. It mobilizes acquired experience by also considering the consequence of the person's culture.

action, even from an emotional standpoint. In recognizing this intuitive component of the decision-making process, Simon also understood its absence from theories of decision making, because it can be seen as a departure from a model of deliberation founded exclusively on calculation. Even if the concept of limited rationality has been recognized by certain researchers, most continue to pretend that it does not exist and believe that it is possible to obtain perfect information, which will serve for making a decision.[7]

To consider rationality as being limited and imperfect, as proposed by the neoclassical economic model, weakens the dominant model and permits catching a glimpse of other paradigms, such as the ethical dimension and the notion of intuitive rationality. According to the neoclassical model, the only important factor in the decision is the determination to take action in order to obtain the best result. Thus, we evaluate the rational behaviour of the decision maker by measuring it against results of the choices he makes. March and Simon open a slight breach in this certitude by examining the process more closely. However, the approach used to evaluate the consequences is sometimes limited to questions of utility or profit.

As mentioned earlier, Simon sees in this process a capacity that favours training. This term must be understood here in the cognitive sense, namely, as training that allows one to understand how information is assembled during a problematic situation and to discover how it is more or less methodically retained in order to resolve other, similar situations. Yet we remain all the same in a very mechanical approach to the decision-making process that separates out each of the actions in keeping with a pre-established sequence. This type of process, in its very structure, corresponds to a closed universe. Emotions are excluded in order to obtain better control, which creates a sort of artificial universe where explanation proves useless, impossible, and even harmful at times. Human actions are stripped bare of their meaning and categorized precisely, as if

---

7. The phrase "perfect information" leads us to understand that we are proceeding according to a substantive reality.

the universe of work were sterilized, exempt from complexity and contradictions. This process does not seem to correspond to a reality that is organic, progressive, interrelated, and interconnected in ways that can be compared to fractal images.

The mechanical conception of the decision-making process can produce a sort of dehumanization of interpersonal relations, resulting in the fracture of all possible ties, because the decisional universe that is proposed suggests a disembodied universe, lacking in emotions, beliefs, and values. It is as if we find ourselves faced with a sort of antiseptic decision, one that exists in neutral territory. In such a universe, moral judgment can only be suspended. As Simon remarks:

> For most problems encountered by man in the real world, no procedure that he can carry out with his information-processing equipment will enable him to discover the optimal solutions, even when the notion of "optimum" is well defined. There is no logical reason for this to be so necessarily; it is simply a rather evident empirical fact concerning the world in which we live—a fact about the relation between the enormous complexity of this world and the modest capacities with which man is endowed to treat information." (1984, 441)

Is it realistic to believe that it is possible to obtain perfect (optimal) information? I do not think so, because all information collection is subjective. Faced with this difficulty, people instead look for solutions that Simon characterizes as *satisfactory*: "Most human decisions, whether individual or organizational, are related to the discovery and selection of satisfying choices." One example is the procedural rationality resulting from deliberations appropriate to satisfying the parties concerned. The definition and application of norms in the process of deliberation can be complex and can force individuals to favour a satisfactory solution over an optimal one (Simon 1997 [1945]). But can the solution be truly satisfactory? And for whom is it so? What are the values that will have been favoured over others that are overridden? According to Jürgen Habermas (1990b), this phase is subject to consensus. In Simon's proposal, which consists of searching for a satisfactory solution, there is persistent discomfort that appears to be personalized. Admittedly, this can be a first threshold of understanding (people get along well, they are in agreement, and therefore they are satisfied), but it seems that this threshold must be crossed.

Decision making is subject to important disciplinary influences. For example, each discipline depends on a conception of rationality adapted to its own research problems. In psychology, for instance, William James (1981 [1890]) defines rationality as being a "process of particular reflection known as reasoning." Irrational behaviour would consist in offering an impulsive response to emotional mechanisms without adequately involving thought. Thus, rationality can be perfect and optimal, according to a neoclassical, limited model (March and Simon 1958), a bounded one (Boyer and Orléan 1997), or a contextualized one (Ancori 1992). Faced with these multiple conceptions, rationality, seen within the context of decision making, is connected to actions, consequences, and results envisaged by the individual or group of individuals.

For example, let us take a situation experienced by most public organizations. Since the 1990s, with the advent of new public administration (NPA), organizations have tended to reduce their human resources (employees) while increasing their tasks. These reductions, especially in public organizations, become more marked under the pretext of heightened rationalization. One sees the subtle burgeoning of far-reaching measures of control that aim to better *regulate* and define the actions of each person. This brings to mind the psychometric tests used for recruitment and employee selection, as well as the electronic surveillance sometimes used to excess to follow their every action and move at work. How can we promote genuine commitment in such an environment of control and surveillance? (See Rosenberg 2005.) Tasks are increasingly subdivided, dissected, standardized, and compartmentalized. Decisions in such a context are justified provided they allow for the improvement and quality of services. These administrative actions and the effect they can have on employees are rarely contested. Everything is justified by economic rationality. In such a context, human beings are seen as an easily moulded workforce from which an unlimited amount of work can be demanded, depending on circumstances. People are called upon to demonstrate greater responsibility and autonomy in their work, because, after all, are they not accountable for their actions? This does not take into consideration the reduced resources and the increase in tasks, which in fact means doing more with less, and the effects of the extra workload on the health of indivi duals.[8] The culture of performance and the climate of generalized competition have repercussions on the health and the morale of workers. It is paradoxical that we have arrived at this conclusion in spite of all the knowledge we have today and the research that has been carried out on the subject of the healthy workplace. On the one hand, we have logic that advocates a revival of paradigms that make room for values, the search for meaning, ecological thinking, concern for the environment, social responsibility, and all ideas and considerations that are fundamentally human. On the other hand, there is the post-positivist reasoning based on financial return and human capital that serves only the quest for material productivity. Such reasoning persists and currently functions to create a certain disenchantment with the world and yet also new perspectives that respond better to today's needs.

Ethical reflection allows us to pierce the fog by imbuing its concepts with value, but it has not yet attained its full force. As stated earlier, ethical reflection demands that we develop new forms of workplace competency, ones that help us acknowledge the uncertain and organic character of situations and take into consideration the contextual aspects and specificities of a given situation while also

---

8. In spite of an abundance of literature on the subject that deals with such effects (Vinet 2004; Brun et al. 2003; Bourbonnais and Mondor 2001), a great deal remains to be done in organizations, and even in the medical field. For instance, the term *professional exhaustion* is not a recognized medical condition, and physicians prefer to categorize this phenomenon as nervous depression. The margin between the terms *exhaustion* and *depression* can be widened, depending on the case.

reconsidering our presuppositions. The first step consists of recognizing the moral reality of organizations, which would, especially, allow performance to be defined in some other way. These observations prompt us to look more closely at ethical decision making.

Models of Ethical Decision Making

Ethical decision-making processes themselves are also subject to the same debate, as there is no consensus on the definition of the notion of ethics, which vacillates between the normative and the descriptive (empirical). However, most models of ethical decision making are founded on the second definitional trend. We will consider only these latter ones.

Models of ethical decision making have existed since the 1980s. These models have been influenced by the work of both Jean Piaget and Lawrence Kohlberg, which relates to moral and cognitive development, and of James Rest, who proposes a process based on four steps: identification of the moral nature of the issue, the establishment of moral intentions, the adoption of a moral judgment, and engagement in a moral action. Most decision-making processes are part of Rest's conception (Rest 1990a, 1990b). Some authors have validated the four aspects of the process and have developed several models. To this approach were added studies that integrated certain variables: genre (Bass, Barnett, and Brown 1999), organizational factors (Treviño and Weaver 1998), and social consensus (Jones 1991; Singhapakdi 1999).

This field of study, which has its roots in the administrative and educational sciences—more specifically in the area of school management—and in moral theories, applied ethics, and psychology, currently benefits from several models of ethical decision making, from a description of behaviour said to be ethical or unethical, and from models of ethical dilemma. Most of the numerous studies that have been carried out employed a quantitative approach that measures dependent variables such as judgment, conscience, moral intent, and conduct, based on demographic variables. The critique that has been formulated in relation to these studies relates mainly to the weakness of the theoretical foundation and the absence of solid hypotheses.

Another important observation: most of the studies used or cited Rest's conceptual framework. Recommendations by researchers of moral and administrative theories suggest going beyond this theoretical framework to bring to light other possibilities in terms of ethical decision making. No critical perspective has been created in respect to this theoretical framework.

Research on Ethical Decision Making
An Overview

Recent literature reports few significant differences in terms of variable type and ethical behaviour. This state of affairs corroborates the research I have carried out since 1997, which upholds the assertion that the presence of ethical leadership does not differ according to type (Langlois and Lapointe 2010). As concerns the number of years and age, some studies (for example, Weeks et al. 1999) show that those who are older and more experienced have better ethical judgment. This observation accords with my studies, which have led to the following conclusion: experienced persons are able to integrate a broader range of ethical dimensions (which include the ethics of care, justice, and critique) and therefore obtain better moral judgments. These three dimensions are noticeable in experienced persons (aged fifty and over). The studies generally confirm that a higher level of education and greater work experience have a more significant and positive correlation with ethical decision making. It is also interesting to note that according to studies on ethics, practitioners are more ethical than students. (Here it must be said that most studies carried out on moral theories and psychology that seek to develop decision-making models or to assess levels of judgment are based on a sample of students in American colleges.) In addition, a significant relationship exists between moral development or ethical judgment and the process of ethical decision making. The work of Kohlberg (1972) shows that the greater the moral judgment, the more ethical the decision.

The locus of control (Rotter 1966), another concept associated with models of decision making, is an important element with regard to ethics. It rests on the belief that our behaviour at work makes it possible to obtain certain rewards (or punishments) or some form of recognition. Some people believe that their success depends on themselves (internal locus), while others feel that it depends on others or external events (external locus). When one associates the locus of control with ethical decision making, studies confirm that internal locus is positively correlated with ethical decision making, while the external locus is not. Studies in psychology confirm that persons who have developed a good internal locus are better balanced psychologically and more able to resolve crises. However, these studies must be approached with some caution, as results are sometimes inconclusive with regard to this notion.

Studies were carried out to determine if deontological codes improve ethical decision making. Most studies that dealt with these two notions support the idea that there is a positive correlation between the existence of codes of behaviour and decision making. Culture, or the ethical climate, has a determining influence on the ethical decision-making process. The mechanisms of reward and punishment also influence ethical behaviour at work. When unethical behaviour is not subject to sanctions or otherwise provokes no response, there tends to be a significant increase in such behaviour in the workplace. An efficient sanctioning mechanism leads to a drop in unethical behaviour.

Moral intensity, which is a recent concept in administrative literature, is one of the elements that can be linked to the ethical decision-making process. Only the studies carried out by Jones (1991) have produced conclusive results regarding this concept. Moral intensity is linked here to social consensus and to a positive evaluation of the consequences for others (magnitude of consequence). Moral intensity affects the ethical decision-making process. Several studies have also shed light on philosophical orientation and the ethical decision-making process. Perhaps more idealistic persons tend to be more ethical than those whose nature is more relativist or individualist. There are still many paths to be explored in terms of ethical decision making. Several studies have highlighted the three final dimensions of Rest's model, namely intention, judgment, and behaviour—while few are interested in the first dimension, namely, moral awareness. What could help people develop such an awareness? To date, we lack conclusive studies about this concept or its development. Furthermore, no study mentions training programs designed to promote better ethical decision making.[9]

The interesting avenues regarding ethical decision making relate to the influence of peers on decisions. Indeed, peers help to curb the negative effects of unethical behaviour and also to better define the stakes. This dilemma is part of the theories on social training. Research carried out by Albert Bandura (1977) demonstrates that human beings learn by observing the behaviour of their peers. This observation is true for both ethical and unethical behaviour. Dimensions such as moral sensibility, judgment, intention, and behaviour differ according to the degree of dependence on peers.

Another interesting notion, which is gaining increasing importance, is that of moral imagination. For the most part, this notion has been defined in proposed models in terms of solutions to be developed and implications or consequence

---

9. The TERA model was developed to fill this gap. Its objective is to help people recognize ethical stakes and consolidate their model of decision making while integrating ethical analysis into it.

incurred. For example, Terry L. Cooper (2006) very clearly identifies the role of moral imagination in the development of possibilities that offer themselves to individuals. Furthermore, Georges Legault (1999) touches on the notion of moral imagination conceived of a capacity to deliberate. We can suppose that it is during the process of deliberation that moral imagination creates a place for itself, although this is not clear from the research.

Morin said about imagination that the individual "temporarily and abstractly enjoys some necessary distancing, a certain detachment, which makes it easier to recognize or understand what is good, bad, pleasant, beautiful, ugly, repugnant, legitimate, etc." (2005, 22–23). In his view, imagination consists in conceiving hypothetical situations and then inferring possible consequences without actually incurring any punishment or personal repercussions.

In decision-making models, moral imagination is never directly addressed, and its process remains abstract. Some research indicates that if people have developed moral sensitivity, they will engage in moral judgment only if they are capable of adequately envisioning several solutions and envisaging what these entail for others (Moberg and Seabright 2000). This process involves moral imagination.

Methodological Considerations

As concerns research methodologies, most of the studies carried out on ethics—over 55 percent in the area of moral theories and administration—used vignettes or pre-established scenarios. As researchers ask their questions based on hypothetical stories, it is easy for the persons being questioned to determine the nature of the ethical dilemmas. Linda Treviño (1998) strongly criticized the use of vignettes, however, because this procedure does not allow for a proper understanding of moral dilemmas. The stories offer an ending that might not correspond to the vision of the participant, as he or she may identify other elements that might allow for a better resolution of the problems. The vignettes and scenarios should therefore be used sparingly and in a stable context, in which certain empirical givens offer solid confirmation of behaviour at work.[10] Another observation relates to research using samples in which 40 percent consist of students to validate results. Much debate has taken place concerning this type of sample, especially in the area of administration, as this does not reflect the reality of administrators or experience gained over time, experience that allows both for the notable improvement of judgment and for possible contamination by the culture of the organization. Also, most of the time, the student is asked to imagine such a situation and to attempt to respond in a hypothetical way. I believe that the use of vignettes with students does not allow for the generalization of data. My results show that experience, age, the size of the organization, and the context are factors that carry a great deal of weight. Beyond the formative nature of this approach, I remain cautious about its general applicability in research.

Most empirical studies use the quantitative approach to measure dependent and independent variables. The use of a technique of analysis depends very much on the theory at issue, as well as on hypotheses or research questions and accessible data. Few studies use mixed techniques capable of evaluating data both qualitatively and quantitatively.[11]

Another aspect, considered quite complex and difficult to execute, is the ability to promote ethical behaviour in comparison to unethical behaviour. The ambition to draw up a complete map of such behaviours proves to be dangerous. However, what is promising is to examine a person in a situation of ethical dilemma, thereby

---

10. The "in-basket" and simulations are interesting exercises designed to initiate an intense discussion and to offer an initial evaluation of moral sensibility. As I see it, however, such exercises do not provide sufficiently rich and complete material to allow for the generalizing of the results obtained.

11. My own research focused on developing qualitative and quantitative tools to better define ethical decision making. I presently have a guide for interviews, a typology for moral acts, and a questionnaire intended to assess the extent to which ethical leadership is being practiced.

raising experimented situations that provide evidence of a conflict of values. This approach allows for harvesting much richer data regarding ethical dilemmas and to define conduct that has been privileged according to a given context.

This analysis, in terms of the dimensions that serve to define an ethical process, allows me to highlight the main concepts presently employed in researching an approach that includes ethics. Furthermore, certain limitations have been mentioned that should warn the reader that, in my view, research in applied ethics is still very young and the methodologies in use deserve careful scrutiny. The models have been developed by researchers such as Bruce Kramer, Terry Cooper, and Georges Legault and by government institutions (see, for example, Citizenship and Immigration Canada 1998). However, these approaches must not be seen as recipes that are guaranteed to result in ethical decisions. Such a view would not correspond to the objectives of the researchers. Each author has created a model based on developments in ethics but has not necessarily considered the professional context in which the research was carried out. Admittedly, the goal of my study also consists in presenting a model, but this model emerges from observations collected from school managers and administrators and from scientific documents that aim to better clarify the process under investigation. The next and final chapter provides an explanation of the TERA model.

Chapter 3

The TERA Model

Towards an Ethical, Responsible, and Authentic Trajectory

The process of moral development is the journey from the irrational and untenable paradise of irresponsible freedom to the lasting and attainable paradise of responsible autonomy.

—William S. Hatcher, *Love, Power, and Justice*, 64

IN THE PRECEDING CHAPTER, WE observed that ethics can be seen as an intellectual discipline offering tools for reflection. Ethics can also be approached from the point of view of a particular language—vocabulary, concepts, methods of reasoning—that enables those who use it to name and study certain fundamental elements of the human experience. Ethics is a process that allows us to analyze the principles underlying a decision and culminates in a specific action. Ethical analysis concerns norms (interdictions, possibilities) that guide human behaviour, as well as values and practical rules that lead us to choose one way over another and moral principles that we strive to respect in terms of our relation-ship to ourselves and to others (Langlois 2004).

The TERA model is part of this vision of ethics, one that aims to discover and highlight elements that will allow for such moral reflection. Ethical questioning is part of an inner attempt to bring moral considerations to the surface. To aid this process of emer-gence, we have listed several questions that can help to set the process in motion:

- What values underlie my decision?
- What goals am I pursuing, and on what basis does my decision rest?
- What do I consider to be just or unjust (good or bad) in this situation?
- What are the consequences for the subject of the action (that is, for the person who undertakes the action) and for others (relatives, communities of interest, society)?

These initial questions provide an entryway into the ethical decision-making process and aim to restore meaning to the term *moral responsibility*. Moral responsibility consists of recognizing oneself as the subject of one's actions and accepting that others recognize this and therefore can ask for an accounting. This is an essential condition for maintaining our sense of identity over time (Ricoeur 1992).

Situations that call for ethical deliberation are omnipresent. Questions come up whenever there is a choice or a commitment to be made, a responsibility to take on. What should I do in this situa-tion? How should I behave? On what basis should I seek support to confront this dilemma? Such questions prompt the intervention of the ethical dimension. It is not just a matter of asking ourselves what should or should not be done (that is, what is good or bad) but also of questioning ourselves about how best to become engaged in this problem and how to assume full responsibility for our actions.

Ethics leads us to envision the implications of responsible commitment. This ethical dimension, understood as a reflective approach, is about taking a personal stand—assuming responsibility and the authority that underlies commitment—in order to learn how to be, as Ricoeur says, the subject of one's own actions. This view highlights the following: ethics is a course of action in which the individual is perceived not as a means or an end but rather as a human being deserving of respect for his or her own humanity.

Why should we be interested in moral or ethical dilemmas? I would argue, for one thing, that someone's experience with an ethical dilemma reveals much about the person's ethical sensitivity. Indeed, we should not assume that all people experience ethical dilemmas. To illustrate the notion of an ethical process, I put into context a situation that involved an important ethical dilemma for a particular person, with the goal of discovering how the decision-making process was approached. During a pan-Canadian research project intended to examine ethical dilemmas faced by administrators, I was struck by the relative absence of ethical dilemmas among those who work in management. Some forty administrators stated that they experienced no ethical dilemmas at work. This result intrigued me. By slightly expanding the scope of my research, I noticed that the organization for which these administrators worked strongly influenced their decision-making process and prevented them from developing a moral sensitivity with regard to the ethical issues they encountered. This blind spot in terms of ethical dilemmas went hand in hand with a lack of decision-making latitude. All decisions had to be justified on the basis of standards and rules established by managers and approved by their immediate superior in the organizational hierarchy. The process of reflection was heavily marked by, and framed within, a well-established bureaucratic model. Although some managers admitted that they felt ill at ease in this structure, they also said that, in the end, the process helped them to detach themselves from responsibility, shifting the burden onto others. Individualism and the lack of an awareness of relationships were very noticeable in this organization.

This result revealed a great deal about ethical sensitivity. Critical issues, such as injustice and inequality, were not discussed or even broached. They were simply ejected by the institution so as not to upset the established order. An analysis of the decision-making process through the exploration of ethical dilemmas thus remains very important for me because it allows for a better understanding of a person's ethical sensitivity.

Moral Dilemma

In philosophy, the notion of moral dilemma is very controversial and raises a number of questions for moral theorists. The most important debate revolves around the following question: What is an authentic ethical dilemma? Philosophers remain skeptical about the existence of authentic ethical dilemma. Some even doubt whether there is such a thing as an ethical dilemma. I do not share this belief. During my research, I met people who clearly stated that they experience ethical dilemmas; they were living in situations where they felt at a loss and expressed their dismay at the behaviour they observed and the injustices that were perpetuated. Ann Davis (2004) confirms that an ethical dilemma is intimately connected with a person's moral identity. What distinguishes a moral dilemma from the resolution of an ordinary problem consists in the fact that a person has difficulty choosing between two important values. There is an internal conflict between the values one holds and the problem at hand, which causes other values to come into play. The solution is not obvious, as these various values are in conflict. Furthermore, all potential action could be harmful in some way. As Hatcher concludes:

> In resolving a moral dilemma, we can do no better than to evaluate carefully the various elements of the interaction, to determine the predominant principles, and then to act accordingly. We will not always succeed, even when trying our best, nor will we always have the time to engage in extensive reflection before acting. (1998, 121)

The study of ethical dilemmas involves the exploration of a confrontation between axiological considerations (the conflict of personal, professional, and organizational values) that, in a reflexive process of calibration, serve to legitimize, temporarily or permanently, the decision of the subject.

In the face of an ethical dilemma, two factors are at issue: the stakes and the ethical choices. By reflecting on a particular ethical dilemma, I developed a semi-structured guide that allows for the detailed study of an ethical dilemma (Langlois 1997). The usefulness of this guide has been validated, and its content improved, over the course of my research.

Ethical Questioning

Ethical questions are raised by the desired results of actions undertaken and the consequences envisaged for oneself and others, which aid our efforts to make a good decision. This introspection engages our capacity for reflection and contributes to moral imagination. The person anticipates several situations, while also weighing the possible positive and negative consequences. Reflection (regarding the outcome of the action) and imagination (anticipation of consequences) are two important elements in ethical questioning.

Ethical Stakes

Attached to the notion of ethical dilemma are situations in which the problem at hand is not clearly defined because values and principles have not yet been established or have not been explicitly laid out. In such cases, there is a risk of ethical dilemmas arising. Taking the time to reflect on the ethical stakes and the goal pursued can help us to resolve the dilemma. A consideration of ethical stakes aims to highlight the values and the various normative standards (or the absence thereof) that bear on the problem, which helps us to understand the situation better. The goal pursued brings to light what is essential with regard to retained value. Reflection relates mainly to an understanding of the broader ethical stakes that need to be evaluated in the context of the immediate problem. What are the anticipated situations? How should we frame (in a normative or regulatory manner) this problem should it come up in the future? What challenges does it raise at the ethical, legal, and social levels? What values do we want to protect? These questions allow for better discernment of the ethical challenges that prevail in a given situation.

An ethical issue is, in a way, a situation that focuses attention on that which could potentially be weakened in the domain of values. What values are imperilled by the situation that has arisen? This question offers the key to an exploration of ethical issues.

Ethical Choices

The sudden presence of an ethical choice provokes questioning and an evaluation of ethical stakes. Ethical choices are not neutral: on the contrary, they convey values and particular standards. In this light, remaining conscious of the fact that our choices reflect one or several normative aspects is important to our sense of empowerment within an ethical framework. The evaluation of choices results from a careful analysis of the stakes involved in a situation. These choices will also bear on principles—prevention and precaution, for example—that mark the actions undertaken or the decisions made by a person, group, or organization.

Ethical Trends

Contributing to our general definition of ethics are multiple currents that have influenced it: Kantian ethics, virtue ethics, consequentialist ethics, and so on. The intention here is not to provide an exhaustive definition of these various approaches: others have already done this. My research has been inspired by the three ethics outlined by Robert Starratt in the multidimensional model he presented in "Building an Ethical School" (1991): critique, justice, and care. This theoretical presentation was part of an ongoing debate that turned on the dichotomy between two ethics, namely, moral reasoning based on considerations of justice (Lawrence Kohlberg) and the concept of care (Carol Gilligan). For Starratt, combining these two conceptions of ethics with an ethic founded on critique constituted quite a challenge, all the more so because, at the end of the 1980s, acknowledging the existence of an ethic of care provoked a powerful debate among moral theoreticians. To complete his theoretical model, Starratt proposed the ethic of critique because of the transformative perspective it provides. I was able to validate his model during my doctoral research (Langlois 1997). The TERA model was inspired by this theoretical construction, and its utility was subsequently confirmed in several research projects and numerous training sessions that involved various organizations and different categories of employees. To understand the TERA model, we must explore the ethical dimensions that will guide this analysis in greater depth.

Three Fundamental Ethics: Critique, Justice, and Care

The Ethic of Critique

The ethic of critique that Starratt proposed is rooted in critical theory, as it developed in the Frankfurt school and was formulated by thinkers such as Theodor Adorno, Jürgen Habermas, Max Horkheimer, and Iris M. Young. This approach seeks to uncover the injustices that one can perceive in social relations or that are created by laws, or that are perpetuated in organizational structures or by the use of language that seeks to obscure the real problem or to render one relationship dominant. In brief, these thinkers sought to uncover situations that benefitted one person or a group to the detriment of others. For Starratt, the ethic of critique aims to discover a whether one group is dominating another and to show how this situation came about so that the injustice can be corrected.

This ethic includes four questions designed to help us understand relations of power: Who benefits from this situation? Is there a dominant group? Who defines the structure? Who defines what is valued or undervalued? When an injustice is discovered, those who adopt this ethical perspective attempt to sensitize others in order to obtain a better balance in the distribution of social benefits. As Starratt notes, "their basic stance is ethical for they are dealing with questions of social justice and human dignity, although not with individual choices" (1991, 189).

The intention of those acting according to an ethic of critique is to ensure that organizational and social arrangements are more in line with the human rights of all citizens. Their goal is also to allow persons concerned by these arrangements to express their opinion and contribute their point of view. The right to be heard can inspire exchanges that are more profound and can bring about changes that make the situation more equitable. The ethic of critique allows every stakeholder to offer whatever suggestions, recommendations, or critiques seem necessary to improve an organization or society. This is, in essence, a form of social responsibility, one that preserves justice and ensures the well-being of those who sometimes find it difficult to make themselves heard.

Organizations offer no shortage of examples in which the perspective of an ethic of critique is relevant: sexism or racism during the hiring process, prejudice towards other cultures or religions, unfair representation on committees (the absence of certain groups), sexist or racist language, the distribution of tasks on the basis of gender, a lack of programs that promote equality, the implementation of policies without any genuine consultation with those affected, the distribution of resources according to ad hoc criteria, access to professional networks or clubs that is restricted to men, and so on. All of these examples raise ethical challenges because they involve unjustified presuppositions and/or offer disproportionate advantages to some to the detriment of others. As regards the existence of such arrangements, those who adhere to an ethic of critique are by no means naïve. As Starratt comments:

> The point the critical ethician stresses is that no social arrangement is neutral. It is usually structured to benefit some segments of society at the expense of others. The ethical challenge is to make these

social arrangements more responsive to the human and social rights of all the citizens, to enable those affected by social arrangements to have a voice in evaluating their results and in altering them in the interests of the common good and of fuller participation and justice for individuals. (1991, 189–190)

Those whose moral reasoning is heavily influenced by an ethic of critique will grapple with the realities underlying choices that might ensure greater social justice. The process of reflection that this approach entails will also bring to light the sort of disproportionate allocation of benefits that can arise when power is misused. This ethical perspective helps us move from a sort of moral innocence, in which we simply assume that this is "the way things are," to a consciousness of the fact that political and social arenas reflect arrangements of power and privilege, interests and influence, that are often legitimized by a supposed form of rationality, as well as by law or custom (Starratt 1991, 190).

In accordance with an ethic of critique, decisions or arrangements are reconsidered in an effort to promote greater equity and justice. The ethic of critique must also be based on the social nature of human beings. The human objectives that the social organization is intended to serve may inspire a manager to promote a sense of responsibility, not only towards the members of the organization but also towards society as a whole. The moral goal pursued by public organizations, such as governments, schools, and hospitals, is to offer the same quality of services equally to all citizens.

The danger or weakness of this ethic is that the critique can become exaggerated and destructive, challenging all decisions and seeing abuse of power everywhere. Given that the word *critique* is preceded by the word *ethics*, it makes sense that, if we are to remain on course, we must pursue a constructive path so as avoid the sort of negative commentary that undermines an organization and creates disunity. Another weakness of an ethic of critique is that it rarely offers concrete proposals about how to reconstruct the unsatisfactory social order. The second ethic, justice, can help us to identify solutions and thus to compensate for the weaknesses of the ethic of critique.

The Ethic of Justice

There are currently two major schools of thought as regards the ethic of justice. The first, according to Starratt, dates back to Thomas Hobbes and John Locke, in the seventeenth century, and finds much of its contemporary expression in the works of John Rawls (1971). Starratt defines this first school of thought as one that puts independent individuals ahead of social relations—which, as they are based solely on the acquisition of certain advantages, were thought to be artificial and governed solely by private interests. The only important values are the interests of each person and individual preference. The social contract of this school of thought is one wherein citizens agree to abandon some of their freedom in exchange for protection from the state. According to Sullivan, social justice is a "social technique which serves to harmonize the needs and desires of individuals autonomously and independently of one another in society" (quoted in Starratt 1991, 192).

The second school of thought, which dates back to Aristotle, can be traced through Jean Jacques Rousseau, Hegel, Karl Marx, and John Dewey and is more in keeping with the concept of an ethic of justice envisaged in my study. It is by experience, by living in society, that each person learns the lessons of morality. This participation in community life teaches people how to view their own behaviour in terms of the greater common good. Civic sense is an initiative and responsibility shared by those who are committed to mutual well-being (Starratt 1991, 192).

According to this school of thought, ethics is rooted in practices within the community. Kohlberg also believes in this manner of learning about justice. For him, moral reasoning and choice were facilitated by a community environment. The protection of human dignity depends on the moral quality of social relations, which, ultimately, is a public and political affair. According to Starratt, in this perspective:

a communal understanding of the requirements of justice and governance flows from both tradition and the present effort of the community to manage its affairs in the midst of competing claims of the common good and individual rights. That understanding is never complete; it will always be limited by inadequacy of tradition to respond to changing circumstances and by the impossibility of settling conflicting claims conclusively and completely. The choices, however, will always be made with sensitivity to the bonds that tie individuals to their communities. (1991, 193)

As one can observe, then, two interpretations are given to justice. In the first school, each person is considered to be a distinct social entity, and social relations are governed by a contract according to which each abandons some freedom for the sake of social harmony. In this view, justice rests on individual choice. In the second school, each person is considered inseparable from society: one's development takes place through one's participation in social life. This training, which is directed at the greater common good, presupposes a certain measure of consultation with one's peers. In this perspective, justice is based on community choice and aspires to equitable governance.

The workplace engages both perspectives on justice: individual choices are made on the basis of a certain consciousness of community, while the choices of the organization are the sum of individual choices made every day at work. An ethic of justice requires the institution to serve both the common good and individual rights. A balance between the two is the goal. How, then, should we govern ourselves? Starratt put this question at the heart of the ethic of justice. Effective governance involves continuous consultation with various stakeholders about policies and regulations. Many organizations have recently turned their attention to crafting mission statements that reflect organizational values. This initiative is an example of a contract that requires the agreement of all. It is interesting to note that, traditionally, the first article of a law lays forth values that will serve to legitimize its purpose. Today, such preambles are avoided.

The goals of an ethic of justice, as advanced by Starratt, is to provoke exchange, to engage people in debate, to demonstrate transparency in management, and to foster consultation and understanding. Those who act in accordance with the ethic of justice aim for responsible autonomy based on cooperation and on the promotion of a just social order within the organization.

A person seeking to foster an ethic of justice wishes to see ethical training activities incorporated into the workplace to foster discussion about individual and collective choices and to sharpen the sensibilities of all. This could mean programs on conflict resolution, value clarification, problem solving, multicultural understanding, and so on. Encouraging exchange on the injustices experienced by persons of different cultures makes it possible to achieve a better understanding and to establish programs that better suit their purpose. Discussions can take place, for example, on the methods of classification and evaluation used by the organization from the standpoint of justice. As Starratt acknowledges, however, none of this is easy: "No doubt such freewheeling discussion of so many taken-for-granted elements of schooling will get messy and unmanageable. Most administrators dread such initial lack of definition" (1991, 194).

Of course, initiating a dialogue on these aspects of organizational life can make some people insecure. We believe, however, that the power of debating what *is* and *is not* allowed in an organization should not be underestimated. There must be very close reciprocal relations between the ethic of justice and the ethic of critique. As Starratt goes on to point out, "often the naming of the problem (critique) will suggest new directions or alternatives for restructuring the practice or process in a fairer manner" (1991, 194–195).

The weakness of the ethic of justice has to do with the effort required on the part of the community to manage its affairs while at the same time taking both the common good and individual rights into account. For some, it is difficult to determine the points of conflict. What is just for one person or group can be unjust for another person or group. Another pitfall associated with this ethic is that it can become bogged down in minimalist considerations. What are the minimal conditions required to satisfy the claims of justice? One should not be afraid to go beyond these minimal conditions and raise the bar. How many organizations have created precedents simply by reconsidering the way things are done and by developing criteria of excellence that were subsequently supported by norms? But in order for the ethic of justice to meet its ultimate goal, it requires the complementary ethic of care.

The Ethic of Care

Starratt bases his ethic of care on the work of Carol Gilligan (1982) and Nel Noddings (1984). Gilligan, in particular, encourages the adoption of this ethical approach from the point of view of psychology. Long associated with the feminist perspective, research on the ethic of care focused initially on the moral development of young women, turning only later to that of men.

The ethic of care relates to the fundamental requirements of interpersonal relations, not from a contractual or legal standpoint but in terms of absolute respect. Starratt adds that this perspective, which is developed through interpersonal relations,

> places the human persons-in-relationship as occupying a position for each other of absolute value; neither one can be used as a means to an end; each enjoys an intrinsic dignity and worth, and, given the chance, will reveal genuinely loveable qualities. An ethics of caring requires fidelity to persons, a willingness to acknowledge their right to be who they are, an openness to encountering them in their authentic individuality, a loyalty to the relationship. (1991, 195)

Those who practice an ethic of care consider human relations to be of major importance to the proper functioning of organizations. There must be concern for the welfare of people in the workplace.[1]

---

1. Of particular note here are the works of Alain Vinet, which deal with the organization of labour and with the health of workers and psychological well-being in the workplace.

The struggle for power must make room for more harmonious social relations, in which everyone works towards common goals. This approach is not about the management *of* people but rather about management *with* people.

This approach to ethics requires that the individuality of the other be recognized. It requires a quality of openness that welcomes each person's distinctiveness; it explores the conditions needed to establish and maintain confidence, frankness, and good communication. An ethic of care goes beyond superficial relationships based solely on legal obligations to establish relations based on esteem, mutual respect, and loyalty.

Several examples can serve to illustrate how this ethic operates in the workplace. Sometimes, relations within an organization include a form of domination or prejudice that blocks all attempts to move towards care, respect, and dignity. As Starratt observes:

> When these underside issues dominate an administrative exchange, they block any possibility of open, trusting, professional communication. Mistrust, manipulation, aggressive, and controlling actions or language on the part of the administrator can lead to a relationship that is hypocritical, dishonest, disloyal, vicious, and dehumanizing. (1991, 196)

An organization concerned with maintaining an ethic of care will establish a culture that encourages the development of harmonious relations. As Starratt says: "Often the use of language in official communiqués will tell the story: formal, abstract language is the language of bureaucracy and of distance; humor, familiar imagery and metaphor, and personalized messages are the language of caring" (1991, 196). Policies founded on the recognition of the individual within the organization and the place that each person occupies express care for others. When a workplace pits individuals against each other, favouring competition and encouraging employees to take on extra burdens, it distances itself from care.

In contrast, workplaces that value people give priority to respect, service, and the spirit of mutual helpfulness. An organization that is guided by an ethic of care values interpersonal relations, the quality of life at work, the health of workers, and the health of the community of workers.

Yet the ethic of care also has its shortcomings. Given a heightened level of familiarity among individuals, it can be challenging to announce a decision that may hurt someone or be a source of concern. For example, a manager who knows that an employee is in the middle of a difficult personal situation might hesitate to share complaints from other colleagues about the person's performance at work. Familiarity between people can also make it hard to view situations in a more global manner. Such limitations can, however, be overcome by applying the other two ethics.

For an understanding of human relations, an ethic of justice requires the profound personal recognition offered by an ethic of care. At the same time, an ethic of justice obliges us to pay attention to the need for greater attention to the social order and to equity. The ethic of critique requires that of care in order to avoid cynical and often depressing expressions of constant discontent. And, finally, an ethic of justice needs the insights offered by an ethic of critique if it wants to look beyond procedural arrangements that ignore the evolution of context. As Starratt reminds us:

> Knowing our own failures to care for others, our own immature ways of rationalizing moral choices, knowing our own reluctance to challenge questionable school arrangements, we are able to confront the general weakness in the human community. Despite our heroic ideals, we often act in distinctly unheroic ways. (1991, 197)

The three ethics reinforce each other to form a holistic approach to analyzing situations. Very complex problems can be examined from the standpoint of what each of these three ethics demands, even if the final decision rests perhaps on only one. This decision can, however, be enriched by applying all three perspectives, while this can also foster greater awareness of the complexity of the ethical problems that arise in the organizational milieu.

The weaknesses of each of these ethics can cause them to depart from the ethical sphere. As mentioned earlier, each ethic has its proper boundaries that enrich and maintain the ethical trajectory overall. When a person acts on the basis of these weaknesses or vulnerabilities, that person is no longer on the ethical trajectory. For example, a manager hesitates in firing an incompetent employee, in spite of negative evaluations, because he knows the individual personally, is a friend of the family, and is aware of the employee's financial situation. Here we encounter a weakness of the ethic of care that overlooks the ethical dimensions of the situation. Turning a blind eye on responsibility, the manager becomes too paralyzed to act and thus perpetrates an unethical practice.

Table 3 highlights the three ethics and the specific moral actions to be undertaken by individuals who wish to remain on an ethical course. My own model for an ethical approach, the TERA model,

Table 3: Moral Actions

ETHIC OF CARE	ETHIC OF JUSTICE	ETHIC OF CRITIQUE
Being present and listening	Righting wrongs	Bringing power struggles and conflicts of interest to light
Developing confidence in social relations and nourishing these	Punishing in a justified manner	Raising injustices and racial, sexual and discriminatory biases
Feeling pain and being troubled by the suffering of others	Offering a well-deserved recompense	Highlighting disproportionate benefits
Ensuring that the person is all right after a conflict	Ensuring that sanctions are proportional to the gravity of the mistake	Uncovering groups benefiting from advantages over others
	Applying rules impartially	

Preserving links and harmony in the organization	Following procedures	Raising consciousness among stakeholders on arrangements, power, privileges, and power struggles
Avoiding hurting others, preserving their dignity	Adopting an impartial and just point of view	
	Establishing equity in exchanges for a mutual advantage	Searching for consensus through deliberation to ensure that what unites triumphs over what divides
According attention to others	Offering equal chances	
Responding to needs	Offering the opportunity to present one's version of the facts	Demystifying technical language used to promote understanding for the purpose of making an enlightened decision
Offering a second chance		
Maintaining open channels of communication	Promoting democratic participation	
Allowing for mistakes	Consulting	
Forgiving	Distributing resources adequately	
	Calling for an investigation	
VALUES	**VALUES**	**VALUES**
Well-being, service, empathy, compassion	Common good, duty, responsibility	Transparency, emancipation, empowerment

© Lyse Langlois 2000

incorporates the perspectives offered by each of these ethics as part of a moral analysis of a given situation. My model rests on three major pillars that together constitute the process of ethical analysis: knowledge, volition, and action. Each of these concepts allows for multidimensional ethical reflection that can serve to better guide decision making.

The TERA Process: Knowledge—Volition—Action

The principle that governs morally authentic general interactions is that we should always act so as to increase our consciousness and awareness of reality. Moral development means a continual enlargement of consciousness and increase in sensibility and awareness.

—William S. Hatcher, *Love, Power, and Justice*, 131

Knowledge

Knowledge is the first step in this process of ethical analysis. It reveals the degree of ethical sensitivity that an individual possesses and makes it possible to grasp the moral dimensions of a situation of conflict and the potential ethical challenges. When one embarks on this phase, ethical reflection engages with the ethical dilemma at hand. This process of reflection is based on the three ethics of care, justice, and critique. The person analyzes the situation by

Figure 1: The TERA model

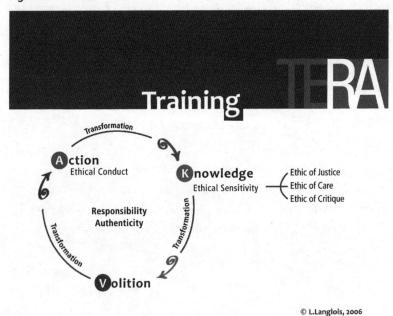

© L.Langlois, 2006

calling consecutively on the three ethics and examining the potential effects that attach to each. This analysis of consequences in the light of the three ethics integrates the dimensions of self, of others, and of the self with respect to others (reciprocity).

The sensibility aligned with an ethic of care requires the capacities for listening, understanding, dialogue, and empathy. Such a sensibility gives rise to a strong awareness of others who are affected by the situation. This ethic derives its legitimacy from a concern for other people and the preservation of their dignity.

A sensibility that places the emphasis on an ethic of justice requires the skills needed to carry out an investigation, taking into account the regulatory framework, while also bearing in mind what is equitable and just. In this context, the person must examine legislative and political measures and procedures pertinent to the situation. The legitimacy of the ethic of justice derives from legal and normative considerations that ensure social cohesion in the light of what is just. Consequences are thus evaluated as a function of this dimension of justice.

The sensibility that rests on an ethic of critique calls for the capacity to sense injustice in language and structure—in other words, to denounce subterranean arrangements (hidden agendas, conflicts of interest, favouritism) that give one group an advantage over another. The consequences are analyzed according to the criterion of greater social justice. The legitimacy of this ethic is rooted in the identification of situations that are to the advantage of some but work to the detriment of the whole.

My research (Langlois 1997, 2004) allowed me to demonstrate that, in the case of any given individual, one of the three ethical dimensions will be more developed than the other two and that most people favour a single approach when examining a situation. In this sense, the "experience" variable is important, as it enables some people to integrate a second and sometimes a third ethical dimension into their understanding of the situation. The integration of the three viewpoints thus often rests on accumulated experience and on a capacity for openness. My research also allowed me to conclude that it is possible to learn and develop an ethical approach that is based on a multidimensional perspective.

During a TERA training program, the knowledge component aims, on the one hand, to help individuals identify their personal ethical viewpoint and mode of analysis and, on the other, to become aware of other ethical perspectives and the consequences of their choices. This multidimensional reflection plays an important role in the development of the sort of ethical sensibility that is central to an ethical decision-making process. This is the path to a clear and well-considered judgment that allows one to become aware of the action to be taken. Knowledge seen in this three-dimensional way enables us to discern the issues more clearly while attempting to bring out the values implicit in each of the three ethics.

Nadine's Ethical Dilemma

Let us take a hypothetical example of a situation that could arise in the workplace, one that involves "Nadine," a human resources advisor who works for a school board.

Nadine noticed an irregularity during an entrance examination for part-time teaching positions in the coming year. One teacher (Teacher A) was offered a position, even though she was less experienced than another candidate (Teacher B), who should have gotten the job. Nadine understands what is at stake: several thousand dollars and additional seniority, not taking into account the possibility that Teacher B could lodge a complaint if she were to figure out what had happened. By analyzing the context of the situation a little further, Nadine realizes that the job is scheduled to start at the beginning of July, when many people will be away for summer break, and that Teacher B will have little time in which to lodge a complaint in an effort to establish her rights and gain the financial advantage. After a certain period goes by, it becomes impossible to file such a complaint. Thus, in view of the holidays, a

July start state can leave other candidates little opportunity to respond.

Nadine's first reaction is to inform her supervisor and suggest that Teacher B have her right to the position reinstated. Instead, her superior decides to let time pass and to say nothing to Teacher B about the situation. Nadine, who is only an advisor, is unable to do anything further. Her loyalty to the organization is shaken, but she decides to side with management. However, on further reflection, Nadine realizes that the decision will place Teacher B at a significant disadvantage. Nadine could very easily close the file and move on, but she cannot resign herself to this. She is faced with a serious ethical dilemma, as she sees that this situation is apparently part of a well-established practice rather than an isolated event. Moreover, by studying the file more closely, she discovers that her supervisor is on very friendly terms with Teacher A.

Framing her thoughts from the perspective of an ethic of justice, she realizes that she will feel uncomfortable if she turns a blind eye. She understands the main elements on which the ethic of justice depends—collectively established conventions, a standard scale for measuring seniority, the assembled facts, and the grievance procedure. She fears that a degree of arbitrariness is becoming the norm and that strategies for evading or circumventing the rules have been put in place in her unit. She wonders how she can turn the situation around justly and equitably. It is at this point that the nature of her ethical dilemma becomes clear. Should she ignore the situation and demonstrate *false organizational loyalty* in order to preserve her place within the organization and the team, or should she strike out on her own and insist that the situation be corrected? Gradually, this ethical questioning becomes part of her thoughts.

The following table synthesizes the relevant considerations and repercussions for each of the three ethics:

ETHIC OF JUSTICE	ETHIC OF CARE	ETHIC OF CRITIQUE
Labour laws, collective conventions, various written policies concerning the posting of positions, and the deadline for filing a grievance	Empathy for Teacher B and others who could be affected in future	The need to divulge the information in a transparent manner so as to avoid creating prejudice or allowing one person to benefit at the expense of others
Deontological code for human resource advisors (integrity)		The need to avoid injustices
The right to appeal		

REPERCUSSIONS ENVISAGED FOR EACH ETHIC:

Ethic of justice: Standards, procedures, and rules have not always been followed in the hiring process for teachers. Such departures risk giving rise to other awkward situations that could damage the organization's reputation and lead to financial loss.

Ethic of care: Lack of understanding and empathy for the teacher who is directly affected by this failure to respect for procedures and the unfairness it produces. The lack of awareness regarding the impact that such a situation has on others will probably cause them to leave the organization and seek employment elsewhere.

Ethic of critique: The re-establishment of an equitable hiring process according to procedure in order to eliminate injustices and demonstrate greater transparency in the allocation of positions.

For Nadine, taking no action would mean acquiescing to an irresponsible and unethical pattern of organizational behaviour, a situation that she cannot tolerate. It is on the basis of an ethic of critique (volition) that Nadine will relieve her ethical dilemma and move on to action.

The following are the sort of questions that participants in the TERA program ask themselves when they engage in ethical reflection: Are people conscious of the ethic they favour? Do they recognize the place of ethics in the organization? Are they able to perceive injustice and inequitable or inhumane situations?

To proceed to the next stage, that of volition, it is essential to have completed the first, that of knowledge.

Volition

Volition is the second stage in the TERA model. It brings to light the axiological dimensions, beliefs, standards, and principles to which we subscribe and determines to what extent we are conscious of their existence. This reveals the degree to which we adhere to such values and the strength of our volition to use them as internal rules. This stage also allows us to determine to what extent we are capable of exercising our free will. It is often difficult to disengage from a problematic situation without yielding to influences or pressure of some sort. The ability to stand back and detach oneself from a situation in order to get a better view of its axiological dimensions proves to be vital. In this way, we are able to pinpoint the considerations that offer essential support for our arguments. To this end, an individual will seek to understand, to exercise judgment, and to choose the value to be defended in a given situation. This stage allows us to determine how far we are willing to defend our point of view in accordance with our principles. It also reveals whether we are motivated to take action to resolve the dilemma while also being able to justify the motives that guide our decisions.

As Linda and Richard Eyre wrote in their bestselling book, *Teaching Your Children Values*, "the wisdom of our predecessors—and our own experience—teaches us that individual and collective happiness constitutes a strong link—if not frankly causal—with behaviour dictated by moral values." Values are linked to morals. As Hemingway put it: "Behaviour is moral when one feels good after the fact. It is immoral when one feels bad." This feeling depends, however, on the degree of ethical sensitivity that each person possesses. Tyrants and criminals feel good after they have committed a crime. Neurological research has highlighted the absence of empathy in psychopaths, who demonstrate no moral sensibility during neurological testing. According to Jacques Grand'Maison, "No one can live without faith. No human society can stand up straight without a minimal conviction to keep it upright" (2007, 12).

Research carried out during TERA training sessions revealed that those who engage in this stage of volition are able to distance themselves from events, and once they have determined their values and legitimized their decisions, they manifest the courage needed for action. Let us return to the previous example, regarding Nadine's ethical dilemma.

ETHIC OF JUSTICE	ETHIC OF CARE	ETHIC OF CRITIQUE
Procedures and rules that are not respected Financial losses Credibility of the organization	Empathy for the person affected by the lack of respect for procedures	Lack of transparency and equity in hiring (injustice)

Do I have the will to act on the basis of the clarity I have gained from these three aspects of my analysis?

Do I possess sufficient motivation to do this? What are the values that will motivate my choices?

Will Nadine use the value of equity to call attention to this situation?

This stage of the model is crucial, for it reflects a person's moral constitution. As it turns out, individuals can feel lost when they realize that they have no truly profound convictions or identifiable values. This stage often leaves them in complete disarray, which prevents them from moving on to take action. The person senses a moral void or a lack of the moral strength needed to act. This moral strength is defined as the capacity to ascribe to oneself robust, constructive, and lasting convictions (Grand'Maison 2007, 12). As William Hatcher observed:

We must therefore strive to maintain the higher view and the broader perspective whenever we are in the midst of our struggle. We cannot succeed unless we are firmly convinced and inwardly resolved that our attempts to act morally constitute the only true and ultimate meaning of our life. (1998, 136)

Action

Several actions have already been accomplished during the previous stages of the ethical process—actions rooted in one of the three ethics. In fact, this last stage, that of action, marks the final decision. At this stage, it is important that we clearly identify the considerations that will serve to defend our position. Before we make any sort of public communication, we must ask ourselves whether our decision will stand up to an in-depth examination by our colleagues, the public, and ourselves. Will we in fact be able to defend our point of view in public and thus pass what ethicists call the media test (Cooper 2006)? Would I still be capable of making and defending this decision even if it were to reach the ears of the media? The following questions help to test our ethical reflections during this stage in the process: Are there any unseen factors that could alter my decision? Am I setting an example? Am I maintaining a bond of confidence with others? Will my decision, which seems just today, seem so tomorrow? Are there particular circumstances that would lead me to make exceptions?

The main skills developed during this stage are moral imagination and judgment, the ability to articulate the two, and steadfastness in terms of choices. When we make our decision, we are sometimes forced to choose between solutions that are equally justifiable and legitimate. Given this complexity, it is important to ground our decisions in what we judge to be solid and worth upholding.

This process, which encompasses the three phases of knowledge, volition, and action, allows us to make an enlightened decision. Such an approach rests on a process of ethical reflection in which we are conscious of the final action we must carry out. An ethical leader is a person who is committed to an authentic process of reflection. The leader seeks to analyze the situation and to gain a global understanding of what constitutes ethical action and then, as a result, will undertake to make a decision that is based on the search for improved knowledge and on volition framed in terms of constructive action.

By taking into account the three ethical dimensions that surround the stages of knowledge, volition, and action, we are able to outline a decision-making trajectory that is both ethical and authentic. These three stages are presented to managers with the goal of enabling them to put into practice a trajectory that is ethical, responsible, and authentic (TERA).

According to André Comte-Sponville (1995), to be authentic means to act in good faith; it means that our words and actions are in keeping with our private convictions and thoughts. As Hatcher comments: "Authenticity leads to autonomy and autonomy to authenticity; each reinforces the other in continual reciprocity" (1998, 124). This reciprocal relationship can serve as a sort of test. Despite being motivated to do so, we may decide at the last moment not to act. Undue pressures can arise, as can doubts about our own capacity to assert our position, which can prevent us from acting. But if we are truly interested in ethics, we cannot be content with good intentions and a desire to *do something* without actually taking any action. Taking action is evidence of a sense of responsibility that shows we have the courage of our convictions. According to Hans Jonas (1990), the concept of responsibility transcends the familiar Kantian imperative. To remain authentic for the duration of the decision-making process sometimes requires that we go beyond the framework of regulations in order to better respond to a particular situation. To be responsible, in an ethical sense, means to be responsible for one's actions and to be able to justify one's choices. As Jonas sees it, ethical responsibility demands that we envisage all the possible consequences of our actions, be these positive or negative, prior to making a decision.

A Challenging but Necessary Interdependence

Man's life depends on his will; without will, life would be left to chance.

—Confucius

The bonds between the three components—knowledge, volition, and action—are not always tightly tied in the actions of those seeking to engage in an ethical process. In my research, I found that *volition* forms the bedrock of the three components, and, for this reason, it stands in the middle of the process. I also observed that tension can be found primarily between volition and action. The passage from volition to action can constitute a significant challenge. It is perfectly possible to identify, in the abstract, what should be done and to perceive it with relative clarity, but it is more difficult to actually carry it out, in accordance with one's sincere sense of determination and one's volition. Each of us vacillates between what can be done—what we can in fact commit to—and a lack of the will to act, which may exist for all sorts of reasons, including lack of courage, conflicts of interest, indifference, and so on.

To sever the connection between volition and action can be a sign of weakness. The separation thus created between the two phases can cause us to abandon the ethical process on which we have embarked. Individuals who were questioned about the gap between volition and action mentioned that personal stumbling blocks—including a lack of motivation—constituted one of the greatest sources of strain. Besides such personal blockages, organizational and structural elements also came into play, such as a work environment that had deteriorated to the point where any action, even that likely to promote improvement, constituted an enormous risk for the employee in terms of career and psychological well-being. When a superior establishes controlling interpersonal relationships with employees, this can also rupture the bonds that exist among the three elements.

Ideally, gaining knowledge of what is acceptable, while considering contingencies, should lead to volition capable of resulting in constructive action. Volition is the link between knowledge and action. The question is, do we need volition to accomplish action? There are several responses. Let us consider a fireman. His training offers him knowledge about what he should do to put out a fire, but is it his instinct or volition that prompts him to throw himself into the fire to save someone? A person who is drowning will be gripped by a survival instinct that will automatically drive him to flail his arms, but it is his volition that will drive him to swim to shore. Without volition, or the capacity to decide and exercise our free will, we are not free.

Our beliefs, our education, and our philosophy of life serve as criteria when we engage in action. I was able to determine that the weakness observed when individuals disengage from an ethical trajectory such as that proposed by the TERA model could be evidence of an underlying void with regard to meaning and values. I observed that people sometimes felt confused during this middle stage in the analysis. They became aware, for the first time, of a certain axiological absence or emptiness when they seemed incapable of carrying out an action or according meaning to their action. For example, if I am in my car and there is a red light, I stop. I know that if I run the red light, I risk causing an accident. Thus, I have the volition to stop. I protect myself, and in so doing, I protect others as well. Volition is the ability to mobilize these personal forces to attain a goal; it involves *motivation, initiative,* and *decision*. It is also at this stage that we see the appearance of courage—the pluck needed to handle a situation and the determination to see it through to the end. In fact, as one of the participants in the TERA research project confirmed, in the course of exercising their authority, some managers attempt to make themselves popular. For her, maintaining ethical behaviour should not form part of a campaign to please everyone. Rather, it requires a dedication to courage, in spite of the traps set in one's way.

The TERA Model: Moving Towards Responsible and Authentic Relationships

The ethical process presented rests on a critical, reflective approach that should allow for (a) the awakening of an ethical sensibility; (b) an awareness of elements of injustice, such as a lack of consideration for others or a lack of respect for rules and regulations; (c) the highlighting of different possibilities, according to the three ethics of justice, care, and critique; and (d) an understanding of the consequences, and the potential consequences, of a decision. The goal of this process is to identify an action that is just and that accords with authenticity and responsibility. By setting such an approach in motion, we are able to distance ourselves from new forms of oppression that alienate the critical spirit and that, in the end, lend legitimacy to social injustice.

A Rising Level of Confidence

There can be no doubt that consciousness or self-awareness is the most fundamental characteristic and defining capacity of the human being.

—William S. Hatcher, *Love, Power, and Justice*, 46

According to Canto-Sperber (2001), an ethical approach must include the following four elements: understanding, knowledge (that is, recognizing what is real), reasoning (anticipating likely consequences), and the specific action, as well as the effect it can have. We see that the TERA model incorporates these four elements at various stages of the process and that, by means of them, the capacities characteristic of the ethical approach are developed.

The first capacity is *ethical sensitivity*, which is kindled by an ethical dilemma. This ethical sensibility is often coloured by a specific ethical orientation, variously associated with care, justice, or critique. For example, it is possible for a person to be faced with an ethical dilemma in a variety of a situations—one that threatens to lead to significant injustice for a specific group, one that could bring harm to someone, owing to the treatment meted out to an employee, one that involves questioning the rules and their application, and so on. An ethical sensitivity represents the conscience that judges these diverse situations. According to Eric Blondel:

> Conscience is in fact the final instance of moral judgment; if it is not the absolute and infallible criterion of the morality of an action, the fact remains that it is the last court before which actions are judged, evaluated, and decided. Without recourse to this last instance of conscience, I am but a blind instrument whose free will resembles that of a roasting spit. (2000, 32)

During one of my research projects, I was able to demonstrate that only the ethic of critique can predict, to a significant degree, the existence of an ethical sensitivity (Langlois 2010). This helps to confirm the importance of this ethic in professional practice. This ethic, which is very close to justice, involves a thoroughgoing social analysis that aims to highlight the elements that prevent the establishment of greater social justice. (Thus we see that the initial action of social movements, such as women battling for equality or those of ethnic and religious minorities, is always driven by an ethic of critique.)

A second capacity is that of *moral imagination*, which is activated during the process of anticipation and the search for solutions, in terms of consequences for oneself and for others.[2] Moral imagination requires depth if it is to allow us a clearer vision of the consequences of a proposed decision. This process demands that we consider several possibilities and assess, in good conscience, what could happen if we were to choose this or that solution to a problem. In this way, one fully becomes the subject of one's actions (Ricoeur 1992) and is able to justify them.

A third capacity involved in the decision-making process is judgment, or *moral evaluation*, which is carried out in the light of one or

---

2. For William Hatcher, "a principle-based ethical system usually underdetermines the individual's response in a given circumstance, leaving room for creativity in the pursuit of moral development. This makes morality a positive and dynamic process, not just a matter of avoiding 'wrongdoing.'"

another possible option. Moral evaluation also requires detachment on the part of the subject so that he or she can better assess all the imaginable solutions. Of course, we can only consider what we are able to understand; we cannot overlook the fact that contingencies may arise in spite of a rigorous evaluation. At this stage, standards, rules, and values are taken into consideration, as are the goals to be pursued. According to Ricoeur, ethics aims to reconstruct the intermediaries between freedom, which is the point of departure, and the law, which is the point of arrival. The area that lies between freedom and the law is that of moral evaluation. Of course, this capacity is not immune from external pressures that might aim to influence the exercise of free will.

The fourth capacity is *authenticity*. To become engaged in an ethical decision-making process requires being true to ourselves in terms of the values we claim to uphold and to be authentic in the relations we have with others. Our behaviour affects others and our working environment overall, especially when we must exercise leadership.

The final capacity is *ethical responsibility*. Philosophers have stated that in order to be responsible, we must answer for our actions. In fact, *sponsio spondere* means to vouch for, to solemnly promise, to commit ourselves to one another and to the law, which requires that we be fully present to others and to ourselves. Questions that come to mind in terms of this last (but not least) capacity are: How should we respond? On what basis should we respond? According to Jean-François Lyotard and Jean-Loup Thébaud, the postmodern age is characterized by the impossibility of judging because "we judge without criteria" (1985, 30). The complexity of today's world has in fact created a void at the level of personal responsibility for making judgments. As a result, we find it increasingly difficult to perform this act, even though we are conscious of the fact that it must be done. In this regard, Jacques Derrida says: "If criteria were simply possible, if the law were present there, before us, there would be no more judgment. There would be technical know-how, the application of a code, the semblance of decision" (Derrida et al. 1985, 94). Responsibility would thus become meaningless because one would no longer have to ask how to make a decision. As de Fontenay (1990) stated, there is no ethical or political responsibility without this test and this passage through the undecidable. Thus, a decision is an experience of the undecidable. This broadening out of responsibility, or this *elastic responsibility*, complicates the experience of the undecidable, because people may shirk their responsibility when faced with a major decision. In an ethical decision-making process, responsibility is bound to volition so that we may find meaning and justifications and thus better understand the real. All the capacities in the ethical decision-making process become blurred if they are not stamped with the seal of responsibility; in its absence, there can be no real ethic.

To embark on a path of ethical reflection, in an effort to practice ethical leadership, can be a major challenge owing to both the pressures under which we now operate and the whirlwind rush into which we are plunged. This state of urgency has become the basic principle that governs our behaviour at work.[3] People are increasingly connected to the immediate moment rather than to the span of time. To find ourselves constantly pushed into this state has important ethical consequences. As the principal function of business problem-solving is to create solutions that work in the short term, this urgency is at odds with the process of ethical reflection, specifically the moral evaluation of the situation, which requires a certain distancing. Today, we no longer engage in this reflection, because the prevailing force of opinion regards thinking about a problem and achieving the distance necessary to evaluate it properly as a waste of time. The needed distancing cannot adequately be achieved because it is increasingly difficult to extract oneself from the here and now. To do more with less is the leitmotif of postmodern organizations.

---

3. Zaki Laïdi (1998) put forward the concept of a tyranny of emergency, or what is commonly referred to as intensification of work.

This cult of urgency has had tangible effects on human relations. Integration becomes difficult, and the feeling of unity becomes increasingly fragmented because individuals are isolated and have fewer opportunities to gather facts or compare points of view. The philosopher Jean Onimus stated that the greater the weight of the economy on our relations and our judgments, the more it will blind us to the lives of others. The pleasures of being together, of creating bonds, of subjecting a situation of moral dilemma to a thorough evaluation before making a choice are difficult to quantify. These are part of another order, that of temporality. Our economic system does not favour this order because it demands too much time.

Our incapacity to engage in ethical reflection, in spite of our desire to do so, produces a sense of urgency, and we feel pressured. Thus the "knowledge" element finds itself conjured away. Those who find it difficult to separate situations from the influences that bear upon them sometimes begin to legitimize situations. They even manage to place them behind a veil to hide their reality. Such legitimacies, sometimes built on false assumptions, constitute major obstacles. The ethical approach aims to delimit new and less porous frontiers, which will serve to preserve the rigour of the ethical decision-making process.

Towards Responsible Leadership

Implementing ethical leadership suggests the importance of thinking critically about the standards and values that underpin our organizations. Such questioning also involves important reflection on extreme situations brought about, for example, arguments that put weight on the normative in order to protect the perpetrator and hide the real causes of improper behaviour. For the manager who attempts to dismantle such legalistic dissimulation, which obstructs the search for truth and prevents sanctions being brought against behaviour that is detrimental to the well-being of the workplace, this can be a veritable obstacle course. For example, a person whose conduct at work is inappropriate or amounts to harassment can benefit from multiple sources of protection before eventually being punished. Sometimes, employees who must work alongside such people can be affected so profoundly that the deviant behaviour leaves them with scars or ends up affecting the overall working environment. Such disruptive behaviour may have endured because of insufficient institutional follow-up, or because no one wants to be responsible for possible interventions, or because the employee was not adequately evaluated. Several managers who demonstrated characteristics of ethical leadership expressed their frustration with such situations. With little or no written evidence to document poor performance at work or behaviour judged to be inappropriate, they must "build a case file." Because this process takes time, a long period passes before sanctions can be applied. The person at fault is thus protected and can continue working with full impunity in spite of faulty performance, resulting in a variety of consequences that affect both co-workers and the organization.

The same goes for those who engage in destructive actions by using dubious means to arrive at their ends. Behaviour that transcends the limits of acceptability and transgresses against norms should be considered unethical. To encourage such actions or to ignore such behaviour means that the manager is likewise supporting a lack of ethics in the workplace. In order to pursue an ethical approach to decision making, managers must be thoroughly familiar with what constitutes professional practice and understand the role and the responsibilities they must assume in order to allow a workplace ethics to take root. When a manager instead covers up the incompetence of an employee because bonds exist that could prove useful or serve his personal interests, he departs from the ethical framework of his job and finds himself standing outside normative standards or in the realm of the unethical.

In the context of the present day, what is needed is critical ethical questioning regarding the limits of the process of humanization and the socialization of behaviour, both individual and collective. An ethic of justice remains vital for governing our collective relationships. However, this ethic must necessarily bring with it a form of questioning associated with the ethic of critique, namely, a questioning of the structures, rules, and foundations that guide us with a view to understanding their social relevance while also taking into account how the context has evolved. Furthermore, certain conditions must be met if we are to bring about a profound change in human relations.

An Ethical Culture

At the very beginning of this work, we raised the idea that ethical leadership in line with a learning organization (Senge and Gauthier 1991), which allows a group to examine its manner of working and to review the benchmarks it uses in its practices. To co-exist, it is necessary to have a common understanding of the norms and values in which our management practices are embedded. In the absence of any real dialogue on values and norms, we find ourselves before an empty organizational shell that does not foster a collective spirit. Ethical leadership is a tributary of this quality of reflection, which we collectively create. This approach requires that the organization provide time and space for reflection and that we distance ourselves from the logic of the market and the pressures that can blur our values. It also requires a certain degree of maturity to initiate a dialogue on sensitive issues that bear on the ethical domain and to learn from our ethical actions in the past as well as from those that were less so.

According to Treviño, an ethical culture rests on values, norms, beliefs, and shared presuppositions that guide ethical behaviour. This foundation raises a whole set of questions about the way of doing things in the organization and the level of acceptance that will legitimize this ethical culture and the norms that surround such practices. During my research, I noticed that several managers who sought to establish an ethical culture in their organization were soon faced with opposition. Their opponents viewed this approach as a disruption of their well-established habits, and they preferred not to initiate such a process of reflection for fear of bringing to

THE ANATOMY OF ETHICAL LEADERSHIP

light certain unacceptable patterns of behaviour that had hitherto gone undetected. To counter efforts to establish an ethical culture, some even went so far as to request union intervention. Changing workplace behaviour or initiating dialogue on values and norms is no small challenge. Different organizations have different levels of maturity and, good intentions notwithstanding, it can be hazardous to try to bring about a change in workplace culture even if it is intended to put ethics at the heart of the organization.

Bringing ethics into the workplace in the form of a critical capacity for reflection requires an organizational maturity that develops only gradually. For some, the process can begin with the establishment of a code of conduct or a declaration of shared values. For others, it can mean revising human resources policy so that it can serve as a beacon for managers who are dealing with a crisis or provide a way to reflect on complex problems experienced at work. Certain conditions are necessary for establishing such a culture: attitudes that elicit individual and collective respect, regard for transparency and clarity in decision making and communication, and rewards for good practices. In brief, maturity begins with a series of actions intended to unite rather than divide, and a set of practices designed to inspire and sensitize people rather than to control them.

The establishment of real dialogue, such as that described by David Bohm, Donald Factor, and Peter Garrett (1991), is the lever that allows for the creation of an ethical culture. William Isaacs defines dialogue as a "shared exploration, a way of thinking and reflecting together" (1999, 9). It is, in a sense, to create something *with* people, to work with others to establish an ethical culture. It is not about a small group of chosen individuals deciding on norms and on what is legitimate for everyone. Establishing dialogue requires changing our way of doing things, which is so often founded on a process of negotiation in which each person must defend his or her position. According to Bohm and his colleagues, dialogue presupposes that perception is privileged over knowledge, the existence of multiple perspectives over compromise, and discernment over decision. In their view, a successful dialogue must include the following elements:

- A temporary exclusion of impulses, value judgments, and so on, which requires exposing our reactions, feelings, and opinions so that our own psyche as well as the other members of the group can see and experience them
- Paying close attention to reactions, impulses, feelings, and opinions so that their structures will be visible the moment these elements appear
- Forgetting hierarchy, because dialogue is essentially a conversation between equals
- Allocating time (at least two hours) so that the dialogue can get going in the group

This practice of dialogue proves essential when, for example, the complexity of situations brings to light considerations that are all equally valid, when unethical behaviour remains vague and difficult to identify, and when there are sensitive areas in the organization that can create situations of crisis.

According to Johane Patenaude (2001), dialogue is a mutually acceptable approximation of the values of truth and justice. It does not necessarily result in consensus but rather is the fruit of a joint process. To engage in dialogue means to accede to the reasonable: one passes from violence to disagreement, from disagreement to questioning, and from questioning to more reasonable questioning. Dialogue requires moving to the level of the object, which is the joint enterprise of sharing meaning, and the subject, namely, the *we*.

This approach to ethics, at the heart of which is dialogue, aims to establish a new moral and social contract, one better suited to meeting individuals' current needs. In the past, ethical principles may have been present but in an implicit manner. With the establishment of ethical leadership, these principles can be articulated and rendered transparent, so that individuals can abide by clear rules when making crucial choices.

In this conception, ethics, instead of being a matter of moralizing to which people must submit, is something they actually live. Such ethics call for initiative and responsibility rather than obedience. Ethics thus becomes an act of responsibility that lies at the forefront of management. This work, carried out in depth, promotes the development of an ethical awareness and sensibility, which are essential to maturity.

If people do not commit themselves to a path of reflection, other, more external imperatives will assume responsibility for formulating conduct appropriate to the workplace and for keeping the public informed: organized citizen groups do not hesitate to demand accountability from institutions. Some even expose behaviour judged to be unacceptable. Without appropriate intervention, this can poison the organization and the work environment. The weight of public opinion becomes important. Numerous non-governmental organizations are engaged in the work of sensitization and in demanding redress in connection with questionable practices. These groups sometimes play the crucial role of watchdog, on the lookout for practices or decisions perceived to be harmful, especially to their community or the environment. In this way, citizens become more aware of both the challenges and obligations of organizations with regard to their roles and responsibilities in the community. Social responsibility is thus gaining ground and is increasingly included in mission statements and codes of conduct. Ethical behaviour at work is of growing concern. External regulations are increasingly common, which contributes to a certain homogenization of behaviour. Such codes of conduct often serve to justify disciplinary measures that are aimed more at ordinary employees than at managers.

At the same time, in some organizations input from employees is invited regarding the values that should govern management practices and inspire people to behave appropriately at work. There is a desire that individuals contribute to defining that which will ensure collective well-being, that will be a source of inspiration, and that will reflect beliefs and values of individuals at work.[4] Objections have also been raised concerning how these initiatives are structured, whence the importance of insisting on transparency throughout the process and when working groups are being set up. If the collective work of reflection is to be productive, it is essential that the team include a representative cross-section of employees. Once a statement of values has been formulated, it must be put into practice in the workplace and subjected to evaluation.

Ethical leadership is not a universal remedy for the numerous ills that afflict the workplace today. However, it is a powerful lever for transformation, one that has as its goal learning how to be and how to live together, rather than instrumental relationships often dictated by accounting, financial, and marketing tools. Ethical leadership, as explored here, allows for questioning the very foundations of an organization and the decisions that govern us.

This transformation enables us to readjust our relationships to accord with an environment that favours autonomy and encourages a constant sensitivity concerning our actions. The paradigm that still dominates our understanding conceives of human relations as inherently conflictual. We must abandon this paradigm so as to make room for management that is better able to build a more human and vital organization.

---

4. I participated in several initiatives involving the development of value statements in both hospital and educational settings, such as school boards and CEGEPs (Québec's colleges of general and vocational education), as well as in municipal government settings (in Québec City).

Conclusion

By focusing on certain aspects of modernity, I sought to call attention to the instrumental rationality that governs most of our decision making. The postmodern period has, in effect, fractured this technical rationality by reconsidering the norms, which has resulted in a return of ethics to the forefront. Because this study rests on data from managers, it seemed important to highlight certain theoretical aspects that, on a practical level, undergird theories of management and administration.

We also explored a concept of ethics that views it as a capacity to reflect on the norms that surround us. In the course of developing an ethics that favours autonomy and free will, I advanced a notion of leadership seen through the prism of ethics. Ideas about ethical leadership evolved at the end of the 1980s and the beginning of the 1990s in the fields of school administration and general management. We embedded our notion of ethical leadership in the ethical decision-making process. In so doing, we called attention to the characteristics of an ethical process identified by researchers working in a variety of fields, from moral theories and philosophy to management and administration. In the light of these considerations, we were able to validate the data we had collected concerning the ethical approach used by managers, mostly in the school sector. We then presented the TERA model, which aims to construct an ethical, responsible, and authentic trajectory at the level of reflection. This approach does not deliver a recipe but rather suggests frameworks within which ethical reflection can occur. The three ethics proposed—critique, justice, and care—articulate the principles that guide this process of reflection.

In light of my research on the impact of training on the ethical decision-making process, I would argue that awareness, or ethical sensitivity, is a determining factor in the adoption of an ethical approach. This sensibility manifests itself in varying degrees, whence the importance of an education in critical thought, so that we will not get caught up in strategies of management or influences that cloud our vision.

Exploring the factors involved in promoting an ethical culture brings us to the next stage in our analysis, one that is of great importance for the creation of an organization that is more human and more sensitive to actions that may be required. We must recognize that inappropriate conduct and the sometimes guilty decision to remain silent about reprehensible actions in the workplace causes ethical suffering. These produce a climate that actually encourages unethical behaviour. Added to this is attenuation of responsibilities, which serves to relieve people of accountability and which also hinders the establishment of an ethical culture.

The major issue raised by individuals seeking to foster an ethical process is the desire for some guarantee that their decisions will be considered *ethical*. By an ethical decision, they mean *an acceptable and just decision*. This issue remains opens, and it calls for a response that rests on norms and values. According to Thomas Jones (1991), the notion of an ethical decision depends on social consensus and on the manner in which people decide whether actions are good or bad. To determine whether an action is good, one must initiate a discussion on the benchmarks we use to judge our guiding professional conduct and practices in relation to what we consider acceptable in a given situation. What is considered acceptable can be defined from both within and without. When the definition comes from outside, we see the work of organizations, community groups, and others who assume responsibility for identifying business practices that place ethical norms at the forefront. It is when the definition comes from within, however, that we have an ethical culture. Policies regarding the management of human resources, the style of administration, and institutional modes of communication create a context that either is or is not conducive to an ethical culture. Among other things, decision making that takes place within a framework of well-defined responsibilities, the existence of clear criteria for evaluating employees, and the development of policies for employee recognition offer powerful incentives for the promotion of ethics in the workplace. Granted, ethical standards that rely on legal norms are more readily operational than those that depend on the articulation of values as well as much more demanding given the preliminary work of reflection that the legitimization of meaning in the workplace requires.

It goes without saying that ethical decision making is part of individual decision making. This fact, however, must not lead us to underestimate the collective dimension that sparks ethical reflection on values and norms that we use to define and justify our actions. The individual is not an isolated being but a social one, bound to others in relationships of reciprocity necessary for authentic ethical action.

This book reflects work in which I have been engaged since I began my doctoral dissertation. This work was intended to define, from within, the moral dimension that surrounds decisions made by people who strive to act properly with respect to their responsibilities and in situations that present them with ethical dilemmas. What was important was to get at the heart of ethical leadership, namely, decision making in a difficult context—a veritable ethical test in terms of the exercise of leadership.

A concrete ethical analysis proves to be a useful method for sensitizing people to considerations that must be kept in view in order to make an enlightened decision. As most ethics researchers would agree, this awareness is the gateway to an analytical approach. Unfortunately, organizations do not often make use of this insight. Of course, the ethic that currently frames most of our relationships is not neutral but is rather embedded in a liberal vision of the market economy and of free choice, one aligned with a rather frantic course of action. Performance at any cost, heightened productivity without regard for the consequences, competition that drives individuals to consider others as enemies—these form the basis of many corporate cultures. Such a perspective has no use for ethical analysis. The fact that, these days, any approach that requires time for reflection is considered unprofitable has created a moral void. Nonetheless, to labour under this yoke is voluntary: it is in itself an ethical choice, one stamped with the seal of liberalism, utilitarianism, and cultural relativism. We return instead to a definition from Paul Ricoeur, namely, that ethics is an odyssey of freedom that lies between blind faith (I can) and an actual event (I do).

Philosopher Hannah Arendt declared that the twentieth century was witness to the banality of evil. Will the twenty-first century instead be marked by awareness and co-operation? We have already witnessed many examples of reconciliation, apology, and the redressing of wrongs. The Maher Arar case is one striking example. After allowing the United States to deport Arar to Syria, where he was tortured as a suspected terrorist, Canada recognized its mistake, presented its apology, and offered him compensation. The stunning and peaceful end to apartheid is another example. Will we see a reversal of other violations of human rights, acts of torture, and repression in our time? Is such ethical awareness not a first step towards increased human maturity?

Having dedicated this book to a very dear friend who passed away far too soon and whose contribution to moral development is beyond doubt, I would like to give him the last word. "The trademark of authentic morality," William Hatcher wrote, "is that it genuinely seeks the moral autonomy and conscious self-motivation of every individual. Moreover, authentic morality affirms that every human being has the capacity and potential to become morally autonomous. Finally, authentic morally asserts that the universal, multi-autonomous pursuit of authenticity will converge to produce a stable but dynamic configuration of society as a whole" (1998, 132).

Appendix

A Guide to Developing a Multidimensional Ethical Conscience

1. Ethical Knowledge: Analyzing the Situation

During your analysis, highlight as many elements as possible that are associated with the ethic of justice and critique. Then make a note of elements associated with the ethic of care that are either present or missing. An awareness of these three ethical dimensions is the necessary first step in a moral analysis of the situation.

Here is a series of ethical questions linked to these three perspectives:

(a) Ethic of critique

Six questions are linked to the ethic of critique; they are intended to assist you in understanding all relations of power or manipulation:

1. Identify the person or persons who benefit from this situation. Identify the person or group who dominates this situation.

2. Identify the person(s) who are liable to be put at a disadvantage by this situation.

3. Describe the forms of injustice that could arise if this situation is not resolved.

4. What are the possible consequences from the standpoint of this ethical perspective?

5. What is the value that you wish to preserve in the light of the ethic of critique?

(b) Ethic of care

The questions linked to the ethic of care are:

1. How do you plan to safeguard the dignity of the person in question?

2. Have you listened to the persons concerned?

3. Do you truly understand the situation from the point of view of the persons concerned?

4. What are the possible consequences from the standpoint of this ethical perspective?

5. What is the value that you wish to preserve in the light of the ethic of care?

(c) Ethic of justice

The questions related to the ethic of justice are:

1. Have you gathered the facts and the means of proof that bear on this situation?

2. Have you examined legislative measures, laws, policies, and procedures that relate to this situation?

3. Do you have the right (administrative or legal) to act or not?

4. What are the possible consequences from the standpoint of this ethical perspective?

5. What is the value that you wish to preserve in the light of the ethic of justice?

2. Volition

This phase aims to bring to light the value that will be preserved and on which the decision will rest. To shed light on the process of ethical judgment, we invite you to consider these questions, which are associated with the second phase:

• What are the values implicit in this situation?

• Which ethic will be given priority in this decision?

• What higher value will be preserved?

• Are you aware of the repercussions and consequences of your ethical choice or your decision? Have you thoroughly weighed the possibility that you neglected to consider a particular ethic (or ethics) in your analysis and the effects this could have?

• What arguments exist to bolster your decision?

• Are you in a position to present these arguments effectively to the public, to colleagues, or to committees and to face a detailed examination on their part? (the other)

• Are you in a position to come to terms with this situation? (yourself)

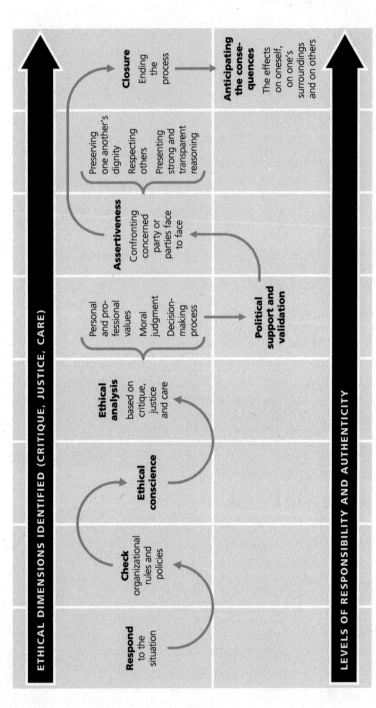

NOTE: Approach adopted by school board superintendents seeking to practice ethical leadership (Langlois 2004).

Once you have answered all these questions, you will have a solid basis on which to justify your action. This justification will give you the courage to act (volition).

3. Action

Describe the imaginary scenario in which you will present your decision, taking note of the fact that all three ethics played a part in your analysis and that, in view of the situation, your decision was founded on one ethic in particular, with the goal of preserving an overarching value.

Questions associated with this phase:

- Will your decision set precedents?
- If so, have you considered the conditions that will be put in place?
- Are you convinced that your decision will be the best and most just in the long run?
- Do you believe that your decision encourages and sustains an authentic and ethical organization?
- Who will be affected by your decision (organizations, individuals, groups)?

References

Ancori, Bernard, ed. 1992. *Apprendre, se souvenir, décider: Une nouvelle rationalité de l'organisation.* Paris: Éditions du CNRS.

Adorno, Theodor W. 1998 [1963]. *Critical Models: Interventions and Catchwords.* Translated by Henry W. Pickford, New York: Columbia University Press.

Arendt, Hannah. 1970. *On Violence.* New York: Harcourt Brace & World.

Argyris, Chris, and Donald A. Schön. 1996. *Apprentissage organisationnel: Théorie, méthode et pratique.* Paris: De Boeck Université.

Bandura, Albert. 1977. *Social Learning Theory.* New York: General Learning Press.

Barnard, Chester I. 1938. *The Functions of the Executive.* Cambridge, MA: Harvard University Press.

Bass, Kenneth, Tim Barnett, and Gene Brown. 1999. Individual difference variables, ethical judgments, and ethical behavioral intentions. *Business Ethics Quarterly* 9 (2): 183–205.

Berger, Peter L. 1999. *The Desecularization of the World: Resurgent Religion and World Politics.* Grand Rapids, MI: The Ethics and Public Policy Center and William B. Eerdmans.

Blondel, Éric. 2000. *Le problème moral.* Paris: Presses Universitaires de France.

Bohm, David. 1996. *On Dialogue.* Ed. Lee Nichol. London: Routledge.

Bohm, David, Donald Factor, and Peter Garrett. 1991. *Dialogue: A Proposal.* Available at http://www.david-bohm.net/dialogue/dialogue_proposal.html.

Boisvert, Yves, Magalie Jutras, Georges-A. Legault, Allison Marchildon, and Louis Côté. 2003. *Petit manuel d'éthique appliquée à la gestion publique.* Éthique publique, hors série. Montréal: Liber.

Bourbonnais, R., and M. Mondor. 2001. Job strain and sickness absence among nurses in the province of Quebec. *American Journal of Industrial Medicine* 39 (2): 194–202.

Bourdieu, Pierre. 1998. The essence of neoliberalism. *Le Monde diplomatique* (English edition). September. http://mondediplo.com/1998/12/08bourdieu.

Bourgeault, Guy. 2004. *Éthiques, dit et non dit, contredit, interdit.* Québec: Presses de l'Université du Québec.

Boyer, Robert, and André Orléan. 1997. Comment émerge la coopération? Quelques enseignements des jeux évolutionnistes. In *Les limites de la rationalité,* ed. Bénédicte Reynaud, 2:19–44. Paris: La Découverte.

Brown, Marvin T. 2005 *Corporate Integrity: Rethinking Organizational Ethics and Leadership.* Cambridge and New York: Cambridge University Press.

Brown, Michael E., Laura K. Treviño, and David A. Harrison, 2005. Ethical leadership: A social learning perspective for construct development and testing. *Organizational Behavior and Human Decision Processes* 97: 117–134.

Brun, Jean-Pierre, Caroline Biron, Josée Martel, and Hans Ivers. 2003. Évaluation de la santé mentale au travail: Une analyse des pratiques de gestion des ressources humaines. Research Report R-342. Montréal: IRSST.

Brunet, Luc, and André Savoie. 2003 *La face cachée des organisations, groupes, cliques et clans.* Montréal: Presses de l'Université de Montréal.

Burnham, James. 1972 [1941]. *The Managerial Revolution: What Is Happening in the World.* Westport, CT: Greenwood Press.

Canto-Sperber, Monique. 2001. *L'inquiétude morale et la vie humaine.* Paris: Presses Universitaires de France.

Citizenship and Immigration Canada. 1998. *The Ethical Compass: Values and Ethics Dilemmas at CIC.* December. Ottawa: Office of the Auditor General of Canada.

Ciulla, Joanne B. 2004. *Ethics, the Heart of Leadership.* 2nd edition. Westport, CT: Praeger.

Coleman, J. S., and T. J. Fararo, eds. 1992. *Rational Choice Theory: Advocacy and Critique.* Newbury Park, CA: Sage Publications.

Comte-Sponville, André. 1995. *Petit traité des grandes vertus.* Paris: Presses Universitaires de France.

Cooper, Terry L. 2006. *The Responsible Administrator: An Approach to Ethics for the Administrative Role.* 5th edition. San Francisco: Jossey-Bass.

Crozier, Michel, and Erhard Friedberg. 1977. *L'acteur et le système*. Paris: Seuil.

Dahl, Arthur Lyon. 1996. *The Eco Principle: The Ecology and Economics in Symbiosis*. Oxford and London: George Ronald and Zed Books.

Davis, N Ann. 2004. Moral dilemmas. In *A Companion to Applied Ethics*, ed. R. G. Frey and Christopher Heath Wellman, 487–497. Oxford: Blackwell Publishing.

de Fontenay, Élisabeth. 1990. Une responsabilité sans sujet. Proceedings of a colloquium held in 1990 at the Collège de psychanalystes: La responsabilité, question pour la psychanalyse. *Psychanalystes: Revue du Collège de Psychanalystes* 37: 34–37.

de Gaulejac, Vincent. 2005. *La société malade de gestion: Idéologie gestionnaire, pouvoir managérial et harcèlement social*. Paris: Seuil.

Derrida, Jacques, Vincent Descombes, Garbis Kortian, Philippe Lacoue-Labarthe, Jean-François Lyotard, and Jean-Luc Nancy. 1985. *La faculté de juger*. Proceedings of a conference held at Cerisy-la-Salle, July 1982. Collection: Critique. Paris: Éditions de Minuit.

de Singly, François. 2005. *L'individualisme est un humanisme*. Paris: Éditions de l'Aube.

Djian, Jean-Michel. 2004. Review of *Où vont les valeurs? Entretiens du XXIe siècle*, ed. Jérôme Bindé. July. Available at www.monde-diplomatique.fr/2004/07/djian/11402.

Dupront, Alphonse. 1996. *Qu'est-ce que les Lumières?* Collection: Folio Histoire. Paris: Gallimard.

Ehrenberg, Alain. 2005. La plainte sans fin: Réflexion sur le couple souffrance psychique/santé mentale. *Cahiers de recherche sociologique* 41–42: 17–42.

Enomoto, Ernestine K., and Bruce H. Kramer. 2007. *Leading Through the Quagmire: Ethical Foundations, Critical Methods, and Practical Applications for School Leadership*. Lanham, MD: Rowman & Littlefield Education.

Eyre, Linda, and Richard Eyre. 1994. *Teaching Your Children Values*. New York: Fireside.

Favereau, Olivier. 1989. Rationalité. In *Encyclopédie de la Gestion*, ed. Yves Simon and Patrick Joffre, 2nd edition, revised and enlarged, vol. 3, 2794–2808. Paris: Economica.

———. 1993. L'économie de l'action collective. In *Action collective et mouvements sociaux*, ed. François Chazel, 251–256. Paris: Presses Universitaires de France.

Foster, William P. 1980. The changing administrator: Developing managerial praxis. *Educational Theory* 30 (1): 11–23.

Galbraith, John Kenneth. 1987. *Economics in Perspective: A Critical History*. Boston: Houghton Mifflin.

Gendron, Claude. 2003. Contributions éthiques et féministes à l'éducation à la citoyenneté. *Religiologiques* 28 (Autumn): 51–66.

George, Bill. 2003. *Authentic Leadership: Rediscovering the Secrets to Creating Lasting Value*. San Francisco: Jossey-Bass.

Gilligan, Carol. 1982. *In a Different Voice: Psychological Theory and Women's Development*. Cambridge, MA: Harvard University Press.

Godbout, Jacques. 1993. *Le langage du don, les grandes conférences*. Montréal: Fides.

———. 2007. *Ce qui circule entre nous: Donner, recevoir, rendre*. Paris: Seuil.

Grand'Maison, Jacques. 1999. *Quand le jugement fout le camp: Essai sur la déculturation*. Montréal: Fides.

———. 2007. *Pour un nouvel humanisme*. Montréal: Fides.

Greenfield, T. B. 1981. Can science guide the administrator's hand? In *Rethinking Education: Modes of Inquiry in the Human Sciences*, ed. Ted T. Aoki. Edmonton: Department of Secondary Education, University of Alberta.

Gunn, J. A. W. 1989. Jeremy Bentham and the public interest. In *Modern Political Theory from Hobbes to Marx: Key Debates*, ed. Jack Lively and Andrew Reeve, 199–219. London: Routledge.

Habermas, Jürgen. 1990a [1983]. *Moral Consciousness and Communicative Action*. Translated by Christian Lenhardt and Shierry Weber Nicholsen. Cambridge, MA: MIT Press.

———. 1990b. Justice and solidarity. In *The Moral Domain: Essays in the Ongoing Discussion Between Philsophy and the Social Sciences*, ed. Thoman E. Wren, 224–51. Cambridge, MA: MIT Press.

Hatcher, William S. 1998. *Love, Power, and Justice: The Dynamics of Authentic Morality*. 2nd edition. Wilmette, IL: Bahá'í Publishing Trust.

———. 2004. *Minimalism*. Hong Kong: Juxta Publishing.

Heifetz, Ronald A. 1994. *Leadership Without Easy Answers*. Cambridge, MA: Harvard University Press.

Hochschild, Arlie Russell. 1983. *The Managed Heart: Commercialization of Human Feeling*. Berkeley: University of California Press.

Horkheimer, Max. 2004 [1947]. *Eclipse of Reason*. London: Continuum.

Isaacs, William. 1999. *Dialogue and the Art of Thinking Together*. New York: Currency and Doubleday.

Jackall, Robert. 1984. The moral ethos of bureaucracy. *State, Culture, and Society* 1(1): 176–200.

———. 1988. *Moral Mazes: The World of Corporate Managers*. New York: Oxford University Press.

Jaggar, Alison M. 1995. Towards a feminist conception of moral reasoning. In *Morality and Social Justice: Point/Counterpoint*, with James P. Sterba, Tibor R. Machan, Alison M. Jaggar, William A. Galston, Carol C. Gould, Milton Fisk, and Robert C. Solomon. Lanham, MD, and London: Rowman & Littlefield.

James, William. 1981 [1890]. *The Principles of Psychology*. Cambridge, MA: Harvard University Press.

Jonas, Hans. 1990. *Le principe responsabilité: Une éthique pour la civilisation technologique*. Collection: Passages. Paris: Éditions du Cerf.

Jones, Thomas M. 1991. Ethical decision making by individuals in organizations: An issue-contingent model. *Academy of Management Review* 162: 366–395.

Kant, Immanuel. 1996 [1784]. An answer to the question, What is enlightenment? In *Practical Philosophy*, edited and translated by Mary J. Gregor, 11–22. Cambridge: Cambridge University Press.

Kanungo, Rabindra N., and Manuel Mendonca. 1996. *Ethical Dimensions of Leadership*. Thousand Oaks, CA: Sage Publications.

Kohlberg, Lawrence. 1972. Development as the aim of education. *Harvard Educational Review* 42 (4): 448–495.

Kuhn, Thomas. 1996 [1962]. *The Structure of Scientific Revolutions*. 3rd edition. Chicago: University of Chicago Press.

Laïdi, Zaki. 1998. Les imaginaires de la mondialisation. *Esprit* (October): 85–98.

Lamonde, Fernande, Lyse Langlois, Alain Vinet, and Jean-Guy Richard. 2007. La pratique d'ingénieurs de firmes conseils œuvrant dans un projet de conception avec intégration de la SST et de l'ergonomie. Projet IRSST no. 0099-4450. Institut de recherche en santé et en sécurité du travail.

Langlois, Lyse. 1997. Relever les défis de la gestion scolaire d'après un modèle de leadership éthique: Une étude de cas. PhD dissertation, Université Laval, Québec.

———. 2004. Responding ethically: Complex decision-making by school district superintendents. *International Studies Educational Administration Management* 32 (2): 78–93.

Langlois, Lyse, and Claire Lapointe. 2007. Ethical leadership in Canadian school organizations: Tensions and possibilities. *Educational Management, Administration and Leadership* 3: 247–260.

———. 2010. Can ethics be learned? Results from a three-year action-research project. *Journal of Educational Administration* 48 (2): 147–63.

Langlois, Lyse, and Hubert Marcoux. 2007. Créer une organisation apprenante pour comprendre le phénomène de l'absentéisme au travail. Unpublished working document.

Legault, Georges-A. 1995. *Questions fondamentales en éthique.* Cahiers de philosophie de l'Université de Sherbrooke, no. 5. Faculté des lettres et sciences humaines.

———. 1999. *Professionnalisme et délibération éthique.* Québec: Presses de l'Université du Québec.

Lenoir, Frédéric. 2005. *Les métamorphoses de Dieu: Des intégrismes aux nouvelles spiritualités.* Paris: Éditions du Livre de Poche.

Lipovetsky, Gilles. 1983. *L'ère du vide.* Paris: Gallimard.

Loe, T. W., L. Ferrell, and P. Mansfield. 2000. A review of empirical studies assessing ethical decision making and the law. *Journal of Business Ethics* 25: 185–204.

Lyotard, Jean-François. 1984 [1979]. *The Postmodern Condition: A Report on Knowledge.* Translated by Geoff Bennington and Brian Massumi. Minneapolis: University of Minnesota Press.

Lyotard, Jean-François, and Jean-Loup Thébaud. 1985 [1979]. *Just Gaming.* Translated by Wlad Godzich. Minneapolis: University of Minnesota Press.

MacIntyre, Alasdair. 1981. *After Virtue: A Study in Moral Theory*. 2nd edition. Notre Dame, IN: University of Notre Dame Press.

March, James G., and Herbert A. Simon. 1958. Organizations. New York: Wiley.

Maroy, Christian. 1997. Rapport à la norme et transformation des modes d'organisation de la production et du travail dans l'entreprise. In *Les mutations du rapport à la norme: Un changement dans la modernité?* eds. J. de Munck and M. Verhoeven, 107–120. Paris: De Boeck et Larcier.

McGregor, Douglas. 1954. On leadership. *Antioch Notes* 31 (9): 66–70.

———. 1957. The human side of enterprise. In *Adventure in Thought and Action: Proceedings of the Fifth Anniversary Convocation of the School of Industrial Management*. Massachusetts Institute of Technology.

Moberg, D. J., and M. A. Seabright. 2000. The development of moral imagination. *Business Ethics Quarterly* 10 (4): 845–884.

Morgan, Gareth. 1997. *Images of Organization*. 2nd edition. Newbury Park, CA: Sage Publications.

Morin, Édgar. 1999. *Relier les connaissances*. Paris: Seuil.

———. 2005. La méthode. Vol. 6: Éthique. Paris: Poche.

Morin, Édgar, in collaboration with A. B. Kern. 1993. Terre-Patrie. Paris: Éditions du Seuil.

Morin, Fernand. 2005. *Pourquoi juge-t-on comme on juge? Bref essai* sur le jugement. Québec: Éditions Liber.

Noddings, Nel. 1984. *Caring: A Feminine Approach to Ethics and Moral Education*. Berkeley: University of California Press.

Northouse, Peter G. 2004. *Leadership: Theory and Practice*. 3rd edition. Thousand Oaks, CA: Sage Publications.

Patenaude, Johane. 2001. L'éthique comme compétence clinique. *Pédagogie médicale* 2 (2): 71–80.

Ramonet, Ignacio. 1995. Les nouveaux maîtres du monde: Pouvoirs fin de siècle. *Le Monde diplomatique*. May. Available at http://www.monde-diplomatique.fr/1995/05/ramonet/1482.

Rawls, John. 1971. *A Theory of Justice*. Cambridge, MA: Harvard University Press.

Rest, James. 1990a [1986]. *DIT Manual*. 3rd edition. Minneapolis: University of Minnesota Press.

———. 1990b. *Guide for the Defining Issues Test*. Minneapolis: University of Minnesota, Center for the Study of Ethical Development.

Ricoeur, Paul. 1992 [1990]. *Oneself as Another*. Translated by Kathleen Blamey. Chicago: University of Chicago Press.

———. 2004. Universal project, multiple heritages. In *The Future of Values: Twenty-first Century Talks*, ed. Jérôme Bindé. New York: UNESCO Publishing/Berghahn Books.

Rosenberg, Richard S. 2005. The technological assault on ethics in the modern workplace. In *The Ethics of Human Resources and Industrial Relations*, ed. John W. Budd and James G. Scoville. An IRL Press Book, LERA Research Volume. Ithaca, NY: Cornell University Press.

Rotter, J. B. 1966. Generalized expectancies for internal versus external control of reinforcement. *Psychological Monographs: General and Applied* 80:1–28.

Salamon, K. L. 2005. Le management par la transformation personnelle: Les nouveaux modes de relation au soi comme moyens de pouvoir et ou de connaissance. In *Gouvernement, organisation et gestion: L'héritage de Michel Foucault*, ed. A. Hatchuel, É. Pezet, K. Starkey, and O. Lenay, 235–252. Québec: Presses de l'Université Laval.

Schön, Donald A. 1991 *The Reflective Turn: Cases Studies in and on Educational Practice*. New York: Teachers College Press.

Senge, Peter M. 2005. Missing the boat on leadership. *Leader to Leader* 38 (Fall): 28–30.

Senge, Peter M., and Alain Gauthier. 1991. *La cinquième discipline: L'art et la manière des organisations qui apprennent*. Paris: Éditions Générales First.

Senge, Peter M., C. Otto Scharmer, Joseph Jaworski, and Betty Sue Flowers. 2004. Awakening faith in an alternative future. *Reflections: The SoL Journal on Knowledge, Learning, and Change* 5, no. 7. Available at http://www.solonline.org/repository/download/Refl5-7.pdf?item_id=8805929.

Sennett, Richard. 2000. *Le travail sans qualités: Les conséquences humaines de la flexibilité*. Paris: Albin Michel.

Simon, Herbert A. 1984 [1976]. From substantive to procedural rationality. In *Models of Bounded Rationality*, 2:424–443. Cambridge, MA: MIT Press.

———. 1994 [1947]. *Administrative Behavior: A Study of Decision-Making Processes in Administrative Organizations*. 4th edition. New York: Free Press.

Singhapakdi, Anusorn. 1999. Perceived importance of ethics and ethical decisions in marketing. *Journal of Business Research* 45 (1): 89–99.

Smith, Adam. 2007 [1759]. *The Theory of Moral Sentiments*. New York: Cosimo.

Snell, Robin S. 2000. Studying moral ethos using an adapted Kohlbergian model. *Organization Studies* 21 (1): 267–295.

Snell, Robin S., Keith F. Taylor, and Almaz M-K. Chak. 1997. Ethical dilemmas and ethical reasoning: A study in Hong Kong. *Human Resource Management Journal* 7 (3): 19–30.

Starratt, Robert. J. 1991. Building an ethical school: A theory for practice in educational leadership. *Educational Administration Quarterly* 27 (2): 185–202.

Starratt, Robert J., Lyse Langlois, and Patrick Duiguan. 2010. Ethical/moral issues in educational leadership. In *The International Encyclopedia of Education*, 3rd edition. Oxford: Elsevier.

Suzuki, David T., with Amanda McConnell. 1997. *The Sacred Balance: Rediscovering Our Place in Nature*. Vancouver: Douglas & McIntyre, and Seattle: The Mountaineers.

Taylor, Charles 1991. *The Ethics of Authenticity*. Cambridge, MA: Harvard University Press.

———. 1992. *The Malaise of Modernity*. Toronto: House of Anansi Press.

Treviño, Linda K. 1986. Ethical decision-making in organizations: A person-situation interactionist model. *Academy of Management Review* 11 (3): 601–617.

———. 1998. Review of *Ethical Dimensions of International Management*, by S. J. Carroll and M. J. Gannon (Thousand Oaks, CA: Sage Publications, 1997). *Personnel Psychology*. April.

———. 2007. *The Key Role of Human Resources in Organizational Ethics*. Washington, DC: Ethics Resource Center.

Treviño, Linda K., and Michael E. Brown. 2005. The role of leaders influencing unethical behaviour in the workplace. In *Managing Organizational Deviance*, ed. Roland E. Kidwell and Christopher L. Martin, 69–87. Thousand Oaks, CA: Sage Publications.

Treviño, Linda K., Michael. E. Brown, and Laura Pincus Hartman. 2003. A qualitative investigation of perceived executive ethical leadership: Perceptions from inside and outside the executive suite. *Human Relations* 561: 5–37.

Treviño, Linda K., and Gary R. Weaver. 1998. Punishment in organizations: Descriptive and normative perspectives. In *Managerial Ethics: Moral Management of People and Processes*, ed. Marshall Schminke, 99–114. Mahwah, NJ: Lawrence Erlbaum Associates.

Vinet, Alain. 2004. *Travail, organisation et santé*. Québec: Les Presses de l'Université Laval.

Wald, George. 1996. The search for common ground. *Zigon: The Journal of Religion and Science* 1 (1): 43–49.

Watzlawick, Paul. 1976. *How Real Is Real? Confusion, Disinformation, Communication*. New York: Random House.

Weaver, Gary R., and Linda K. Treviño. 1998. Methodologies of business ethics research. In *The Concise Blackwell Encyclopedia of Management*, ed. Cary L. Cooper and Chris Argyris. Oxford: Blackwell.

Weber, James. 1990. Manager's moral reasoning: Assessing their response to three moral dilemmas. *Human Relations* 43 (7): 687–707.

Weeks, William A., Carlos W. Moore, Joseph A. McKinney, and Justin G. Longenecker. 1999. The effects of gender and career stage on ethical judgment. *Journal of Business Ethics* 20 (4): 301–313.

Young, Iris M. 1996. Communication and the other: Beyond deliberative democracy. In *Democracy and Difference: Contesting the Boundaries of the Political*, ed. Selya Benhabib, 120–135. Princeton, NJ: Princeton University Press.